# OPTIONS VOLATILITY TRADING

# OPTIONS VOLATILITY TRADING

## STRATEGIES FOR PROFITING FROM MARKET SWINGS

## ADAM WARNER

New York   Chicago   San Francisco   Lisbon
London   Madrid   Mexico City   Milan   New Delhi
San Juan   Seoul   Singapore   Sydney   Toronto

ISBN    978-0-07-162965-2
MHID   0-07-162965-3

*Printed and bound by RR Donnelley.*

This publication is designed to provide accurate and authoritative information in regard to the subject matter covered. It is sold with the understanding that neither the author nor the publisher is engaged in rendering legal, accounting, or other professional service. If legal advice or other expert assistance is required, the services of a competent professional person should be sought.

—*From a Declaration of Principles jointly adopted by a Committee of the American Bar Association and a Committee of Publishers*

McGraw-Hill books are available at special quantity discounts to use as premiums and sales promotions, or for use in corporate training programs. To contact a representative please visit the Contact Us pages at www.mhprofessional.com.

*To Susan, Jamie and Josh*
*for your love and support.*

*To Mom:*
*In my thoughts.*
*Always.*

# CONTENTS

# INTRODUCTION

Volatility affects all types of trading, whether you ever lay your eyes on an options screen or not. This book will both help deconstruct some commonly held myths about options and volatility, as well as teach readers how to manage and profit from them.

Awareness of the whole concept of volatility has grown by leaps and bounds over the past decade. Unfortunately, so has the misunderstanding of what it all means. *Options Volatility Trading* will show you how to best measure volatility and how to manage an active account or an investment portfolio in a world of ever-changing risk premiums. And you might actually have some fun doing it!

Numbers? We've got numbers. You will learn some factoids about The CBOE Volatility Index, affectionately known as the "VIX" that you never even thought to ask. What days of the week or the expiration cycle might make sense to look for certain types of trades? What happens to volatility at different times of the year or around holidays? Or on different days of the week?

You will see plenty of data suggesting different seasonal plays, ideas of what to do when volatility does "X" and the put/call does "Y," and so on. But this is not a systems book; it's a concepts book. We're not here to just give away the fish, as if there was such a simple fish to begin with. We're here to teach you how to fish—minus an overabundance of fishing and hunting and poker-playing clichés like the one I just used.

Don't get me wrong, I love to read studies along the lines of, "When we see such and such backdrop, the market has risen 14 of the last 17 times over the next two weeks," and so on. The trick though is not finding and exploiting pot odds like these; it's handling trades and positions when you get those rare outliers.

I frequently omitted 2008 as part of my statistical work. Why? Well, partly because I would waste everyone's time putting a caveat on every statistical observation with, "If we eliminate 2008, we see a very different picture." Consider this one big caveat. Including 2008, of course, provides the most complete and correct picture—if our only goal was to produce a series of hard and fast rules. It's not. We strive more for guidelines, knowledge that perhaps you throw into your tool set when making trading decisions in any given market.

Volatility analysis always revolves around an assumption of mean reversion, that is, a tendency of moves in one direction to ultimately "revert" to some sort of perceived "mean." But mean reversion is an amorphous concept. The same way that there is no one single correct Price-to-Earnings ratio or price-to-book valuation or any valuation metric, there's no correct VIX. Sure, we can get average and median readings over any time frame. But means themselves fluctuate. The year 2008 was about a worldwide diversion from the mean of any and all asset classes. The lesson to me was not that rules stopped working but rather it was that we should always be cognizant that rules *can* stop working at any time. And we need to trade and invest accordingly.

Volatility proved no different from pretty much any asset class. The key to earning money, or even staying afloat, in 2008 was not adherence to any sort of probabilistic system but rather ability to recognize precisely that heretofore reliable systems were all on tilt.

Many VIX and generalized volatility observations in the book confirm anecdotal observations from my 20-plus year career in trading options. But many debunk them as well. And to some extent they debunk what seems like common sense. Buy-writing was, is, and will probably always be the most popular use of options. Since that involves shorting an option, common sense says that it behooves the trader to sell at an objectively "high" volatility. But that may ultimately prove misguided from many angles. We will explore when buy-writes work best, in the expiration cycle and in certain moves in volatility.

We make a brief tour through Greece, or rather through options Greeks, in order to make sure that the foundation is nice and solid for some more advanced options and volatility concepts. But fear not. The math rarely borders on the complex in these pages. And that is by design. Nothing makes my eyes gloss over more than words like "Gaussian" and "lognormal." And trust me, many have made a nice living in the options business without ever even hearing words like that.

We also stray off the volatility and options path to discuss and analyze brand spanking new options, like products that hit our shores in 2007 and took off with a bang in 2008—leveraged Exchange-Traded Funds (ETFs). If ever a vehicle should have a sticker on it that says "for trading purposes only," it is Direxion and ProShares line of leveraged products.

But before we begin, let's get one thing perfectly straight. Volatility and the VIX have become one big blank canvas at which market participants have thrown all sorts of qualities as the whole concept of tracking and trading volatility has taken off. Just remember first and foremost, the VIX is *not* a stock.

Volatility is simply a statistical calculation. Similar to how your PC translates a bunch of 1s and 0s into what you see on the screen, a volatility reading simplifies a sometimes complex standard deviation formula. And the VIX takes it one step further and expresses the volatility of one single product, the S&P 500 index, as an easily accessible number. There's truly no particular magic here. The VIX and volatility in general provide us with a wealth of information that we will parse and hyperanalyze from every which angle. You will walk away from this book way better equipped to analyze and trade all things volatility.

So join me as we travel through the wild and wonderful world of options trading.

# OPTIONS VOLATILITY TRADING

# Chapter 1

# WHO AM I?
# WHY AM I HERE?

## So Who Am I, and How Did I Get Here?

Well it's 1987, and I am one of the rarest of birds, a prospective Johns Hopkins University graduate who did not plan to go to medical school.

OK, I exaggerate. Fully half of us had other pursuits in mind. Mine was Wall Street. I had experience as a floor trader. A little bit. The NYSE (New York Stock Exchange) had opened up a tiny options exchange and populated it with free seats to anyone owning an American Stock Exchange seat. And at the time, my father owned just such a seat, so he set me up for a summer of floor trading before my senior year of college. It worked out well in that I somehow ended up in the black, without really knowing a whole lot as a 21-year-old novice. But more important, it would serve as good résumé filler as I looked to get a "real" job somewhere in the finance industry.

I went with the "strength in numbers" theory and sent out my info to any name or address I could find. And I got a handful of interview requests, some of which went comically bad.

There's the interview a friend of the family got me, with a muckety-muck at Salomon Brothers. It turns out that a crucial bit of information goes unmentioned, namely that way back 20 years earlier, my father fired this guy from a now-defunct brokerage firm. Revenge must have felt sweet, as this muckety-muck proceeds to ask me all sorts of technical options questions about theoretical modeling and whatnot. And when I can't answer, he tells me I lack "intellectual curiosity," which I imagine was an accurate observation at the time, although I have successfully traded options for 20 years and probably would still have trouble answering whatever it was he asked. I was tempted though, at the end, if he asked if I had questions, to say yes. Then in my best Stephen Wright voice, ask him, "If you are in a car traveling at the speed of light and turn your headlights on, what happens?"

Then there's the interview I lined up with First Boston somewhere on the East Side. I grew up in New Jersey and had a couple summer jobs in New York City, but they were always in the financial district. So I had quite limited familiarity with the NYC subway system and an extreme underestimation of the width of Manhattan at about 50th Street. Long story short: I took a subway train that landed about four long city blocks west of my destination, and I had about five minutes to walk the difference. This experience resulted in a very sweaty interviewee.

Miraculously, though, I did land a job with a great firm called The Options Group. No trading, but it had a growing online presence in the options valuation field. *Online* meant something very different in 1987, of course. It was a hard-wired, Microsoft, DOS-based, dedicated system installed on several of the big trading desks around the world. The company dealt with not just equity options. In fact that was its smallest footprint in the business. It was the de facto pricing mechanism used by pretty much every large currency desk at the time. Instead of negotiating a trade via price of the actual options, currency traders negotiate by volatility and then use The Options Group's system to generate the actual price.

In other words, Trader X at Credit Lyonnais agrees to sell $1 million worth of some yen/dollar ATM option with three months until expiration to Trader Y at JPMorgan at 15.2 volatility. Both traders, with our system on their desk, plug in all the specifics, and out pops the price JPMorgan will pay.

In 1987, that was magic. And for me, it was a great way to make contacts at a bunch of trading desks.

The Options Group has four principals, one of whom is Joe Sullivan, one of the founders of exchange-traded options trading. It's a great group and a perfect match, except for my actual job description. I work in technical support, which means that any time a customer has a complaint, I get on the phone with him or her (or go to his or her office) and try to fix the problem. Not exactly what I wanted to do with my life.

As I get ye olde résumé ready again, my father asks if I want to just trade on the AMEX in the meantime. I always knew that I had that opportunity as a backup, but at the time I really wanted a regular job. But for whatever reason, I took him up on the offer.

It turned out to be a terrific decision, though it took a couple years to pan out.

## I'm Going to Walt Disney World

When someone thought of floor trading back in 1988, the first thing that came to mind was that last scene in the movie *Trading Places* where 500 guys and Eddie Murphy and Dan Akroyd scream and make hand signals in some sort of organized mayhem. And at a scrawny 5 feet 7 inches tall with a soft voice and rather relaxed manner, I hardly fit the ideal profile. Fortunately, that's not how an options market worked; it followed a more civil procedure.

Basically, every options class had a specific post where it is traded, and on the AMEX, there is a dedicated specialist. Market makers then came in two forms: crowd traders and boat people. Crowd traders stood in one spot, the same spot every day, and made markets in one or several options classes. Boat people moved with the order flow.

They'd go wherever it was busy on a particular day and then try to scalp some profits out of the order flow, ultimately flattening out their positions when it quieted down, and they then moved on to the next busy situation.

I chose the former, and picked the Disney crowd to start my AMEX life. It seemed like a good spot. My father had traded there as a member, and everybody knew him so I figured I'd be like a "legacy" or something.

The problem is that this is not how the floor works. You see back in 1988 on the floor, you have an edge to just about every trade you put on. And you, the new guy in the crowd, simply walk in as a dollar sign to the existing traders. A negative dollar sign, as in every contract you do is one fewer they do, and since back when floor trading had real pricing advantages, that contract translated into money out of their pockets. So they want to make your day as uncomfortable as possible. Not quite like when they locked George Costanza out of his office in a *Seinfeld* episode, but uncomfortable enough.

An options crowd on the AMEX worked like a pretty well-oiled machine. The markets on the screen are all established and maintained by the specialist. Traders in the crowd generally say that they are on all the markets on the board, and they then give their size. Say "20 up," meaning you will buy 20 on every bid and sell 20 on every offer. Technically, as the markets change, they must reestablish. Let's say that the stock ticks down, and the specialist lowers all the calls $1/4$ point (we traded in $1/8$s and $1/16$s at the time). The crowd traders must then say something like, "Out of my x bid in the Jan 60 calls, 20 offered at y". But the reality is that established traders in the crowd never have to do that. It's just understood that they are on the new markets. For the new guy though? Not so much. If an order comes in, they may try to stick you with the whole trade at the old price or not include you on a trade at the new price. Things like that. You're the only one held to the letter of the law.

And let's say a big order comes in, call it 1,000 contracts. And it's a good trade. And there are six other traders in the crowd. They'll all have leeway to increase their size and take down their full share of the trade, probably about 100 contracts. But you'll be limited to the 20 contracts you stated before the order even came in.

What's more, they'll keep trades from you as best they can. Go get a pack of gum? Magically 100 calls always trade on the bid while you're gone. Meanwhile if one of them steps out for a smoke, he or she will get included on the trade when he or she returns.

Don't even try to extend a hand of graciousness. You're going to get a cup of coffee, and you want to see if anyone else wants some. You're wasting your time. It could be 10 below outside, and they have the biggest caffeine headache known to humanity, and a broken leg to boot, which would mean they'd have to crawl out and get the cup themselves, and they'd still turn it down. They. Want. You. Gone. Period.

But it's just a right of passage. They ultimately have no choice. You need to prove yourself as an upstanding crowd trader. By this I mean that you have to be there to take down your share of the clunker trades as well as the good ones. You have to contribute some degree of thinking, like offering an intelligent opinion on how to price a spread or whether the volatility on the board should go up or down and so on. You ultimately get into the club. And once you do, the shoe now goes on the other foot, and you're the one trying to make life uncomfortable for the next guy who wants in.

## How about a Quick Time-out to Clear Up Some Misconceptions?

The AMEX has (or had, maybe I should say) three types of options members: brokers, who handle orders for third parties and could not act as both agent and principle; market makers; and specialists. Market makers and specialists both ostensibly provide liquidity and depth to the marketplace, differing mainly in that specialists get awarded (or purchase) the right or obligation to make markets in certain products (known collectively as their book). Specialists make money primarily by trading, but at one time they also collected commissions on orders they handled through their book. That latter part became more and more negligible over the years. And even in the best days, it didn't generally cover their overhead of trading memberships, technology, and clerical employees. Market makers strictly participate in the liquidity and depth part, but they have far less overhead to cover—really just the cost of the seat.

As I said, the job is to make markets for customer order flow under many restrictions. Bid/ask spreads always legally needed a certain depth and maximum spread. This was a bit loosely enforced, however, as market conditions often dictate wider options markets.

If a customer comes in and asks for a quote in a certain option series, the specialist owes that customer a "fill" (an executed trade) on either the bid or offer, up to a certain quantity. When I began, the exchanges all guaranteed only 10 contracts on every bid and offer. But over the course of time as liquidity and competition tightened everything, exchanges guaranteed fills on up to hundreds, or even thousands, of contracts, depending on the specifics of the product. For example, QQQQ, the Exchange Traded Fund (ETF) that tracks the Nasdaq 100 Index, guaranteed super tight bid/ask spreads and super large quantities on either side as the underlying ETF was always as deep as could be. Conversely, a singly listed inactive equity option would come nowhere close to that.

Of course specializing/market making was not an altruistic business. Far from it. We were there to rake in as much as we could.

Before I get into things that maybe we did do to help us along, let me dispel a myth about something we were often accused of but never actually did—manipulate markets.

For some reason, any time a trader/investor sees a call not go up as much as he thinks it should in a stock rally, or a stock expire at a price he dislikes, he immediately accuses market makers of somehow jiggering everything to personally hose down his position.

First off, let the record show that market making is a reactive business. Your job is to make two-sided markets. When an order comes in, you take the other side of it. Your edge is your bid/ask spread. If a customer sells calls, you generally buy them at or near your bid. And if a customer buys them, you sell at or near your offer. Some orders are smarter than others, and the trade will not look so good by the time you write it up (that's a polite way of saying that there's a lot of smart wired money out there). But over the course of time, if you make intelligent markets and hedge with discipline, you generally come out ahead.

But the trade-off for that edge is that you don't pick your positions; you just have the opposite position of the order flow on that particular product.

So if you're convinced that someone manipulated something, perhaps the first place to look is the party that initiated the trade to begin with.

Second, the relative size of the players is misunderstood. If an order comes in to sell 1,000 calls, there's one party on the sell side, probably an institution or hedge fund. On the flip side, the "crowd" maybe consists of seven traders buying 100 each, and a specialist buying the remaining 300. And the market makers then likely go hedge by selling stock, collectively adding some shares to the offer, and probably moving the stock lower. Hedging more aptly describes this action than manipulating.

But who actually moved the stock? The customer selling the 1,000 calls to begin with. And it should be noted that it's not at all illegal on the surface. If she sold those calls knowing there was a size seller in the stock already, then perhaps we have a case, although a case I never saw brought up in 13 years on the floor.

Mark Wolfinger from *Options Trading for Rookies* traded on the Chicago Board Options Exchange (the CBOE) in a time period overlapping mine, and he tells a similar tale:

A reader suggested that I occasionally pass along stories of my days as a CBOE floor trader (market maker). He was especially interested in whether market makers manipulated the markets to their advantage.

Anyone who peruses online forums knows that market makers are blamed for many things. Included in the list of accusations: stock price manipulation, charging outrageous prices for options, dropping prices just when customers want to sell options, etc.

Things are quite different today than when I was a member of the Chicago Board Options Exchange (1977 through 2000), but I'll do my best to tell you how the world of the market maker looked from my perspective.

### Manipulating Markets
I never heard of any market maker being able to manipulate markets. I did hear a story of how one market maker responded to an influx of option orders by unsuccessfully attempting to affect the stock price. He lost a pile of money in the process.

The unfortunate part for me is to read or hear about customers who believe that the market maker took advantage of them. Instead, the reverse was true. Large customers, such as the brokerage houses with their own trading departments . . . frequently "picked off" the market makers by buying a bundle of call options moments before a large order hit the NYSE floor to buy shares in the underlying stock. I don't want to make accusations in writing, and we had no evidence of the illegal action of "front running," but we always felt that these companies knew about the buy order that was headed to the NYSE. Thus, they bought call options for their own account, anticipating that the stock price would jump, as a result of the pending buy order.

Afterward, we would write reports, make accusations, but all for nothing. No one was ever punished and we were frequently the proud owners of a "short delta" position as the stock was rising. Somehow, we were never able to buy stock fast enough (in an attempt to hedge our option sales) because that large NYSE order arrived on the trading floor before ours. The world moves much faster now, and I assume this problem no longer occurs.

In my opinion, market makers did not routinely (I use this word because I have no way of knowing if it ever happened) take advantage of customers. Instead, it was the big customers who took advantage of market makers. But people who make accusations on public forums would have no way to know that was happening—and I doubt many would believe it was true.

Just as customers blamed market makers, we market makers blamed customers. Perhaps no one ever did anything wrong and it's just human nature to blame someone else when a losing trade is made. But, I find that difficult to believe. Placing blame truly depends on your perspective.

I never heard any inside information; I was never the recipient of any news. And by the time I heard anything, the rest of the world already knew about it. Our edge came from being on the trading floor where we could see options orders before others. In today's world, that's no longer true. Every big order is "shopped" off the trading floor before it is ever shown to market makers.

Third, floor trading is heavily regulated. Trade on a floor, and your exchange and 16 regulatory bodies or so will follow your every transaction.

Let me share an example that may help illustrate this point.

One of our options in the mid to late 1990s was Duracell, the battery maker. A very slow option, nothing much happens. Then all of a sudden, call buyer after call buyer walks in. Volatility explodes. With no calls for me to buy anywhere, my only defense involves overbuying stock. But I can't buy stock one for one, lest I get incredible downside risk should the call buyer prove completely wrong.

Long story short, the call buyer's bunny had a good nose. Gillette bids for Duracell, and the stock flies much higher. Thanks to all the stock I bought, the loss I take is "human." And I ultimately recouped as the SEC froze the call buyer's account, which turns out to have been wired through somewhere offshore. The buyer incidentally chose to forgo his illegal profits in return for never challenging the charges.

How did the AMEX handle it at the time?

Well, a day or two after the stock explodes, I get a call from upstairs. I'm asked why I exercised my At-The-Money calls the month before.

Yes, I kid you not. With the expiration cycle before the market had the first whiff of a Duracell takeover, the Duracell stock closed right above strike. And I owned calls at strike, presumably against an otherwise short position. So I exercised them and filled out the proper paperwork as the AMEX required us to do any time we had an expiration "exception." Options automatically exercise when they are in-the-money, but in-the-money in the mid 1990s for a market maker meant first $1/4$ in the money, then $1/8$ of a point. If, say, Duracell closed at 50 $1/16$ and I owned calls with a strike of 50, I needed to formally exercise them if I so chose. And then I needed to fill out a form with the AMEX, because this was deemed an "exception."

Similarly, if it closed at 50 $3/16$ and I wanted to not take my automatic exercise, that was an exception too.

So anyway, here I am, picked off blind in Duracell for real money, and the AMEX is calling me to task for an innocuous and logical options exercise a few weeks earlier. I imagine I made my displeasure known; I did not see the humor in it until later.

Basically, in the exchange hierarchy, a market maker (MM) represents the lowest form of subspecies. Order providers are the bread and butter, and rules and protections serve them and their customers first and foremost. The brokers who represent them often (always) get the benefit of the doubt if they can convince someone they acted in the customers' best interests. Specialists have the power structure in their favor in that they are the biggest players on an exchange, but the flip side is they often sit on the wrong side of a dispute in the exchange's eyes. Market makers are necessary evils and have little say in anything.

Did MMs cheat? Of course. It was never a choir over there, just not in the way or scale of public perception and more at the expense of another trader who maybe was entitled to a trade that someone else took.

In today's world, the market maker barely exists, particularly the independent one. Time was, the options exchanges teemed with people on percentage deals where a larger trader or trading unit would back a bunch of traders and spread them throughout the floor. The general deal was a monthly "draw" against an escalating percent of the profits they generated. Maybe they'd pay a trader 50 percent of the first $100,000 he earned after expenses, then 60 percent of the next $100,000, or whatever. The trader might also draw out a $2,000 or $3,000 or whatever guarantee each month against her net profits.

## Those Days are Long Gone

The few left standing (now sitting) in a crowd, be it a real crowd or a virtual crowd, generally just serve as employees for a larger organization—a simple salary and bonus situation. Most are young and would probably take it as an honor that pundits think they have either the will or the means to move a Fortune 500 company around at their beck and call. But it's frankly a laughable construct.

## And Now Back in the DeLorean to 1988

Pretty much every option is traded on only one exchange, so you had exclusive market making ability, which made buying everything on your bid and selling everything on your offer a much better business model.

Some orders came through automatically on something called the "Dot" system, but most were through brokers who got them from their on-floor clerks who got the orders via their phone lines.

You would stand in a crowd and make a trade with a broker, and then you would write down the details on a little red or black pad. A clerk from your clearing firm would pop by every hour or so to collect the tickets and input them into the system to be matched up and cleared the next morning.

Needless to say, waiting that long to find out potential "don't knows" (called DKs) could cause huge problems.

If you had to hedge with stock, good luck. You called your NYSE broker. Or rather you called the broker's clerk on the NYSE. At some point your order hit the floor and maybe got executed. You wouldn't really know for sure until it traded "through" your price, the actual "report" didn't come back for as much as an hour. Even when it went through, it was often not clear whether your order made it on time. If there was some question about whether you got filled or not, you could call the clerks, but you really could pester them only so much. Confirmations on their end were generally verbals (spoken information) from the actual broker.

If it was a big trade and you really needed to do a stock trade and fast, you had some issues. The specialist had a *huge* advantage; he or she had a direct wire to a broker and a clerk who could handle the order while you were busy giving your "name" and other info to the executing AMEX broker and then elbowing the other traders to get your name on first so you could get to the phone. (By "name" I mean your badge and clearing house, not your actual name. I was "Wagner 855W" at the time, later we all had unique three-letter acronyms.)

If your underlying stock was a Nasdaq name, you really had a rough go of it. ECNs (Electronic Communication Networks) didn't exist yet, so you were at the mercy of some Nazz dealer. You needed real edge in any Nazz option to offset the fact that you were getting smoked on any stock execution.

Want to change your option bids and offers? Today you can just set a volatility and a spread and a size, and a machine will update automatically with each tick. And you can do that while you're sitting in a Starbucks in Vermont or anywhere. In 1988 the specialist would have to tell an exchange employee known as a "reporter" what exactly the specialist wanted changed. The reporter would then fill out a card and pop it in some machine that seemed like state-of-the-art back then.

## How Exactly Did This All Turn Profitable?

I've laid out the disadvantages of floor trading—the fact that you become a sitting duck as you get forced to fill "smart" orders, the problems you had in the earlier days getting hedges off, and the competition between traders and between traders and specialists.

If we could only get rid of that last one, maybe the business model would work.

And lo and behold, in the days before wildly improved automation and dual listing of every product, competition within a floor was not as intense as met the eye, or at least the perception of what met the eye. Again, everybody had (and probably still has) a *Trading Places* view of what goes on at an exchange.

But the fact is that options trading crowds develop a clublike structure. You tended to work together far more than you worked in opposition—and together with the specialist as well. Your profit potential was that spread between the bid and the offer in every series. If an order came in with a limit between the two, you have a strong incentive to act on it in unison as opposed to acting in competition. However, you had to earn your way into the club structure of each crowd; you could not just walk in and expect to be a part of it. You needed to demonstrate basically that you were a standup person and would take the good with the bad and not cherry-pick the best ones.

Now, of course, like any form of trading, it involves a luck element and a skill element. The best trader on the floor might just stumble into a spot that simply doesn't work. Suppose you get a big call seller, and you keep buying and getting longer and longer calls and shorter and shorter stock as you hedge. And then you suffer a subsequent crush in volatility. There's not an awful lot you could do way back when as the concept of cross-hedging via index product option shorts was just not something anyone but the bigger shops could do. You were cooked.

Conversely, the worst "me too" market makers might latch themselves onto a winning situation, say that same order flow as above, except this time volatility happens to explode, and a position they can barely conceptualize earns them a mint.

Let's assume that the vagaries of order flow will even out over time and that each crowd has an equal chance of getting lucky or unlucky. Frankly, your best path to profitability depended on the ability of the specialist to handle order flow and the degree to which the crowd and specialist avoided stepping on each other's toes.

Let's say for argument's sake that an order comes to sell 1,000 at-the-money calls in stock XYZ. And it's a predecimal and predual listing (so the company can't go to some other exchange and get a market in the same name) The broker will say something like, "How are the XYZ Jan 50s?". The specialist, speaking for the crowd as a whole, maybe says, "5 to $^3/_8$s, 100 up," meaning that the market is 5 bid for 100 contracts total, 100 contracts offered at $5^3/_8$. And we'll assume that market is correct, meaning that the "fair" value of the calls, based on where the stock is right here, right now, is $5^3/_{16}$.

The broker, with 1,000 to sell maybe says "1,000 at $5^1/_8$." In theory a trader or specialist could buy some or all of these right now. They're worth $5^3/_{16}$ as we said, so you could sort of lock in $^1/_{16}$. I say "sort of" because it depends on shorting stock right here, and it's not clear you can do that given that a 1,000 lot of ATM calls for sale means you need to cumulatively short 50,000 shares against it (remember we said they are ATM, so we'll assume it's a 50 delta (each call is equivalent to 50 shares of stock)). It also depends on your volatility being correct, and it's highly likely an order to sell 1,000 ATM calls will have the effect of lowering the implied volatility across the board. So the 6 cents or so you potentially lock in can turn into a loss at lightning speed.

A good crowd, and by good I mean profitable, will work together handling this order in many ways. The first thing you likely do is show a fill somewhere other than on your bid. Together. Maybe you say "5 bid for 100, $4^7/_8$ bid for the balance," or something like that. Again, you need to sell stock to hedge, and you need to account for the fact the volatility will surely decline the moment the print hits the tape. Second, you will probably all offer stock at or above the current offer. If you sell that stock, you are now in the driver's seat because you can either buy the calls and lock in the trade or use the calls as a "stop" against the stock you sold. And then maybe you bid for the stock lower and just flip for a profit without ever trading the calls.

And in a good crowd, if you decide to buy some calls, you buy your share, in other words, the number of calls you would buy on a split if they all traded at once. Let's say there are seven traders in the crowd, all play in equal size. Your "share" of the trade will be 100 each, while the specialist does the remaining 300.

## So How Would This Work in Practice?

Let's say stock XYZ is 50 bid, $50^1/_4$ offer. The call seller walks in. I know that I can do 100, which means that to hedge, I need to short 5,000 shares. So maybe I offer half of that to start, 2,500 shares at $50^1/_4$, and the other half at $50^3/_8$.

Now suppose I sell my stock at $50^1/_4$. I am in the driver's seat. I can take (buy) 50 of the calls and lock in the trade. I can take my full 100 and leg the rest of the stock I need to short. That is, try to get a better price on the balance of my stock offer while risking that I don't ever sell it. Or I can do nothing with the calls and take my chances that the broker changes the limit down, and that could very well happen, because if it looks like we can sell stock, we can now bid more aggressively on the calls, maybe 5 bid for the whole 1,000. Or the stock simply declines, and I buy back my 2,500 shares cheaper.

All contain paths to profitability. The big risks are (1) the broker cancels or crosses the order *after* I sold my stock, or (2) the broker sells us the balance of the calls, and I've only half hedged or not hedged at all with stock, and I have trouble shorting. Both may lead to scratch or moderate loser trades as I either have to buy the stock back in scenario one or short more lower in scenario two, aided by the fact that we bought the calls at a good price.

As time went on, order shopping became more common, and the ability to "sit" on an order and flip stock against it diminished. You had real risk of someone from the outside swooping in and buying ahead of you. But in reality, you knew those players too. And it was in everyone's overall interest to be somewhat cooperative as this situation popped up over and over again. So you tended to cede some of the quantity of the trade.

As you can see, a good crowd afforded you many "heads you win, tails you scratch or barely lose" setups.

## How about a Bad Crowd/Specialist?

A bad specialist may get too aggressive. He or she may take the entire lot of calls then and there, or bid 5 for the whole 1,000. In either case you pretty much have to participate in full. As part of the "club" you could voice your disagreement with the bid, but fail to participate and you probably face a day or two of getting shut out on further trades. Do it too often, and you're pretty much out of the club.

Getting back to the trade—it sounds great in that at the time you "lock in" $3/16$, but in reality this leaves you very susceptible to a smart order. In other words, if the broker sells you the calls right then and there, and next thing you know, the stock implodes before you short any. And as you learned, often the hard way, if a broker instantaneously hits a bid or takes an offer with a size order and doesn't have another customer in hand already bidding for it, then it's a smart money order.

A trader in the crowd not playing with the team might just take some or all of the calls himself or herself, in which case you make or lose nothing, but you have forgone an order that maybe makes you some money. And for that trader, it's going to become a zero sum or losing sum game to keep doing that, for the reasons we lay out above. He or she is probably locking in a mediocre to poor volatility *if* he or she gets short stock off.

So assuming luck was just that, luck, and skill was self-defined, the real key was finding a spot with good order flow and an intelligent crowd that did not tend to shoot at each other.

## Nothing Lasts Forever, Even Cold November Rain

From the moment I began, in 1988, I was told that it was just a matter of days or weeks or months until the floor as a business went away, thanks to technology making us all superfluous. Well it happened eventually, but it was more like years.

Automation improved gradually over time. Yes, that allowed me to enter stock orders via handhelds, as opposed to the veritable "two dixie cups and a string." But it also wildly increased the transparency of our markets and the ability for someone from the outside to see and trade off our markets. Order shopping increased, so the ability to "work" an order all but evaporated because you never could sit on anything anymore.

But still the business worked. In fact I would argue the late 1990s were the best of times for options market making.

Seat rental prices provide the best barometer for the profit potential of floor trading. Membership on the AMEX (or any exchange) requires owning or renting a seat. The sale price can fluctuate because of many factors some of which depend on the ability to earn money as a member, but some of which have nothing to do with that, such as the value of the real estate underfoot, or, in later years, the value of the exchange itself as a for-profit company.

The rental price however reflects the profit potential of a member—what someone will pay for a month or a quarter or a year of the ability to make markets. Not all deals are the same because the length of the agreement, flexibility to break the contract, and so on varies, so it's tough to get an exact price at any given moment. But in the late 1980s, that cost something like $1,000 to $2,000 per month. By the late 1990s, the price rose as high as $16,000 to $18,000 per month. And there was excess demand, so much so that I remember a trader whose lease was about to run out walking around the floor with a sign attached to him asking if anyone had a seat for rent.

But then August 1999 came, and with it, dual listing of all existing options.

At some point in the 1990s, all new options products were listed on every exchange, so the Yahoo's and Netscapes and Qualcoms that came down the pike all traded everywhere. But existing names like Phillip Morris and CAT and Pfizer and, well, most everything, traded in one spot in the United States. And if for some reason it listed somewhere else, it was a clear secondary market without order flow. Much, if not most, of the floor advantage was in controlling the execution of orders.

The options business stayed good for another half-year or so, basically the time remaining on the tech bubble, not to mention the volatility bubble. It took us half a year to notice that "edges" were gone and we were effectively still profitable only because as a floor trader you perpetually own options volatility. The most popular options trade was, is, and will probably always be the buy-write. We get into this in depth in Chapter 12, but as it pertains to the floor, it implies that if you stand in a crowd and take the other side of order flow, you will likely own most calls on the board at one point or another. Whether a customer executes the trade as a package with stock or a stand-alone call sale against stock he already owns, you the trader generally buy those calls and immediately or eventually short stock against it, thus producing a long gamma and long volatility position.

To make a long story short, as long as the market kept rallying and volatility stayed strong and elevated, it still seemed as if the business "worked." The problem was that this all ended, and next thing you know you have a bunch of extra products thanks to the fact that you were now listing every option in the United States and you had no edge in any of them. Options brokers and options customers now had the upper hand. The days I describe above of having the ability to work orders were gone And were replaced by a broker playing one exchange off another.

The specialist first reacted by trading super aggressively, maybe taking some profit-and-loss hits so as to keep order flow on the AMEX. All a broker had to do was breathe and she got a fill on an order, no matter how big or how difficult it was to hedge. I can almost pinpoint the situation that made me realize I really couldn't stand in a crowd any more. I was making markets in Juniper (JNPR) one of the hottest of the hot in the latter stages of the tech bubble. The stock traded in the 300s; options volatility was maybe 80–100. It's a perfect spot to trade small and wide. Yet our specialist had his own agenda; he wanted to aggressively court order flow and was happy to use our capital to help him in that cause. So basically anything that traded was split up, be it a 10 lot where we each got one contract, or a 1,000 lot where we took down 50–100 each. And as long as something was within the market and within reason, he traded it.

And when you bought or sold 50 or 100 Juniper contracts in 2000, you were essentially just rolling dice where you might get stock. You were lucky to scratch; more often than not you scrambled.

And with that I decided I had had enough. This would only get worse. Automation and competition were improving as the Internet Stock Exchange and it's fully "virtual" exchange came on the scene, as did decimals, further tightening bid/ask spreads. Standing in a crowd involved a bit of a trade-off even in the best of times because the edges you got working and even just seeing orders was often offset by the fact that many orders were a bit "wired" into what was about to happen in the stock. But with spread edges essentially gone, why stand in a crowd and take the other side? You always had a random position; now you have a random position with no price edge in your favor putting it on to begin with. If I am going to trade options, I might as well decide how I want to sit. It was time to go.

For every trader really, within a few years, seats literally went down to 0 to rent on a couple of exchanges as you still needed to pay fees as a member. And the business became even more automated. The CBOE morphed into a hybrid model where part of the membership was virtual. In other words, you could participate as a market maker from a remote location just as if you were physically present.

## Where Are They Now?

Go on the AMEX today, and it's almost like a library. You still have some market makers, but instead of eight people standing in a crowd, you now have maybe one or two. And they're not standing; they're sitting at a sort of counter, almost like at a diner with a laptop wired in. They may physically sit 3 feet from the specialist, yet they also may not even utter a word to one another because all but the biggest spread trades execute automatically. The trader can just pop her markets in automatically. She could be sitting anywhere in the world and do the same thing. The physical options exchange has become an anomaly; it still exists only because it existed to begin with. You would never start a new one; it's all automation now.

And the AMEX itself will be gone by the time you read this as it is slated to merge into the NYX/NYSE/Archipelago/Euronext Borg, formerly known as the New York Stock Exchange.

It of course makes sense, but it's a shame nonetheless.

## Now What?

Perhaps it's now time to learn less about me and the history of the physical options exchange and more about options themselves—maybe a tour through Greece—the options terms unfortunately, not the country.

# Chapter 2

# KNOW YOUR GREEKS

I am not a big stickler for requiring knowledge of every last term. It's more important that you understand the risk and reward picture of an individual option or combo of options than to know exactly what to call those attributes. But it doesn't hurt to learn them. For instance, can you trade options successfully without knowing "Greek" speak? Well, you will not get quizzed on Dionysius or etymology or anything of that sort, but if you want to read a value sheet or analyze your positions or allocate capital, you will need to learn a thing or two about a handful of Greek terms.

Making matters more confusing, many terms have dual meanings. A Greek can refer to both a characteristic on an individual option and an aspect of your entire position in a class, or even an entire portfolio. So let's dig in on a few of them.

## Delta

*Delta:* The amount an option's price will change for a corresponding one-point change in the price of the underlying security.

Simple enough. In other words, let's say the Exxon (XOM) April 75 calls have a 60 delta. If you own one April 75 call in XOM, it equates to your owning 60 shares of XOM. But we also use delta to refer to a position itself. If you own 10 of these XOM calls and have no other position, you might say, "I'm long 600 deltas in Exxon," or something like that.

And this is an important concept to internalize. Let's say that XOM is trading at $77 right now, and you buy 10 of these XOM calls for the price of $6.50. There are two ways to look at and allocate capital to this position. One way is to look at the total dollar value committed and risked to the XOM position. Let's say we run an account of $100,000. We bought 10 calls for $6.50 each, so that comes out to a net outlay of $6,500, leaving us with $93,500 more to play with. That $6,500 is all you can lose on XOM, but from this viewpoint, the position has enormous leverage. Suppose XOM declines by 1 point, a mere 1.3 percent dip. The calls have 60 delta, so they will theoretically drop 60 cents in value. That's a total of $600, or roughly 9 percent of the initial investment. If we had 10 or 15 other similar positions in our account, our portfolio could drop 5–10 percent on one pretty plain vanilla unexceptional market dip. That's leverage.

The other way to look at the XOM? Convert those calls to a stock equivalent position, and allocate according to that. Use your total dollar outlay as a de facto embedded put on the position. Those "600 deltas of XOM"? Allocate as if you actually own the XOM. So 600 shares of a $77 stock means that you own the equivalent of $46,200 shares of XOM, which implies that you have room for only one more play like that in a $100,000 account.

Now it's not exactly like you own that much XOM. You paid only $6,500 out of pocket for that right. If XOM closes at or below 75 on April expiration, you will not exercise your right, so ergo you will not lose more than that.

That's your embedded put.

To me, some blend of the two approaches, with a tilt toward the latter, makes the most sense. Because after all, what if, say, we also buy

10 Freeport-McMoran Copper and Gold (FCX) May 20 calls at $6.50? If we were allocating simply based on our dollar outlay for the position, we would have a pretty randomly constructed portfolio, to be polite.

FCX trades at $24, and the calls have a 75 delta, so after converting to deltas, that $6,500 investment would get us long the equivalent of $18,000 of FCX, under half the exposure of some dollar investment in XOM.

So as you can see, before expanding onto more complex options analyses, you at least need to line up the relative sizing of a portfolio of options positions like these.

## Gamma

*Gamma:* The rate of change of the delta for a $1 change in the price of the underlying asset.

Again, that's the basic meaning. Let's say that the XOM options above have a gamma of about 3. That means that for every 1 point lift (drop) in XOM, the delta of the calls lifts (drops) by 3. So if XOM goes to 76, the calls now have a 57 delta; if XOM goes down to 75, they have a 54 delta, and so on. Obviously that 3 gamma does not last forever (the calls never get to negative delta, or over 100 delta, to make the obvious point), but we'll stay away from third derivative stuff for now.

And like delta, gamma has a broader meaning when applied to an entire position. Someone might say something like, "I'm long 600 deltas in XOM with 100 gamma." That's the basic way an options trader looks at her position. If XOM lifts $1, her positional delta increases by 100. So now she's long the equivalent of 700 shares of XOM. If XOM lifts $2, she will presumably be long 800, and so on. And scratch that and reverse it on the downside. Down $1, and you are only long 500, and so on and so forth.

How might one get a long gamma position? The simple answer is to buy straddles or strangles. Buy either one and you get longer on the way up and shorter on the way down. But really any position that is net long calls or long puts has a positive gamma component.

Positional gamma is a hugely important metric that dictates how aggressively we can trade and hedge a specific position. But it's not the be all and end all. Best to also keep track of the simple number of contracts net long or short in a given name. You may have an ostensibly positive gamma position that is positive only around a relatively small price range. Maybe you have a spread on where you are long some calls near the money but short many more calls out of the money and not in play right now. But what happens if the stock lifts a bit? That positive gamma will roll into negative gamma really fast, so it's best not to aggressively hedge the position.

As a floor trader, you end up with all sorts of complex positions that look and behave differently over different time frames. Your clearing service, and then later your handheld device, could spit out a net delta and a net gamma position at a moment's notice. But that might not tell you everything. I always found a "line count" valuable. I would literally handwrite how many contracts I net owned or shorted at each strike price, maybe separating out near month/near money options if we were close to expiration. With an involved position, you have a purer picture of what may or may not happen should the stock move.

## Vega

*Vega:* The rate of change of the options' value with respect to a one-point change in the volatility.

Vega is not actually even a Greek letter. But it is probably the most important risk associated with options — and the most difficult to grasp.

Basically, the volatility of an option is not cast in stone. It can change overnight. Literally. I started trading options in 1988, so I missed the crash, and I would say I didn't quite appreciate the power of vega until about 2000 or 2001. Don't get me wrong, we always accounted for it, just not an overnight move that can maybe change the value of Long Term Equity AnticiPation Securities (known as LEAPS) options $1 or $2.

Take Google (GOOG) for example. With the stock at $340 at the beginning of February 2009, Jan 10 350 calls trade at a 44 volatility. That's a pretty middle-of-the-road level for GOOG options in early 2009. So I wouldn't expect them to move too far too fast.

The vega however is 1.25, meaning that all else being equal, a one-point pop (drop) in volatility would cause a lift (decline) of 1.25 in the value of the calls.

Now to put it in perspective, these calls trade with a 57 full. But even so, a one- or two-point volatility move is pretty common, and having a position on the wrong side of one of those moves and having multiple contracts affected can really add up.

Like all other Greeks, traders also quote vega in relation to an over-all position. Something like, "I have 400 vega in GOOG." Translated to English, this would mean that the trader stands to earn (lose) $400 for every one-point lift (drop) in GOOG volatility.

Caveats aplenty however — almost gamma times 10, or 100 in terms of the way a basic positional vega number can mislead.

Vega is *very* unequal across time frames.

GOOG March 350s, with about seven weeks to go, have a vega of .48. GOOG Sept 350 calls, with seven — plus months until expiration have a 1.06 vega. On the flip side, the nearer to expiration, the more volatility will fluctuate. So March options might lift or drop 5–10 volatility points before Jan 10 options even move a point in volatility.

A "one-stop" positional vega reading will simply conflate them all and tell you what happens when they all go up or down a point. And that's a problem, because all cycles will not move at the same pace.

Let's say you own the Jan 10–March 350 calendar 10 times. Your plain vanilla vega reading will be:

[(vega of the Jan 10s you own) – (vega of the March 350s you are short)] x (number of contracts) x 100

Throwing in the numbers from above, it comes out to 770—which is saying that a one-point lift in volatility will net you a $770 profit. Sounds great—or bad if volatility declines a point and the reverse happens. But here's the catch: It won't happen like that. A one-point move in the Jan 10s is large and, like we said above, probably associated with at least a five-point move in the Marches. And if that's the case, you stand to lose (earn) more like $230 per one-point volatility lift (drop) in March options.

So if you look at the vega of a position, the best thing to do is a separate analysis of each expiration cycle. You may end up rooting for something very different from what a combined vega tells you.

## Theta

*Theta*: The rate of change of the options value as time (one day) passes with all else remaining the same.

This definition is for one single option. For example, those GOOG March 350 calls have a theta of .22. This means that tomorrow those calls will have a value 22 cents less than they have today, all other things like stock price and volatility remaining equal.

And instead of theta, most people simply refer to it as "decay."

But as they do with all of theta's Greek friends, traders use the term more broadly to refer to the decay of an entire position in one name (like "my daily decay is $220 in Google). They even use theta to refer to decay in their entire portfolio. And at the end of the day, option trading is all about managing vega and theta. Let's say you have a play on where you net own options, like a straddle or strangle. A pure volatility long. You will necessarily now have a position with negative theta (negative decay). Your position gets you longer into strength and shorter into weakness, which sounds great. But that negative theta represents what that "great" costs you each day.

Your goal is simple. Earn more from that position each day than you pay in decay. If you have a GOOG position with –220 theta, you need to earn over $220 off the position each day in order to pay for that decay. How do you do that? Well, you need to either flip GOOG stock or ride your position well enough to make that money back. That number represents daily decay. But we have these things called "weekends" and "holidays" where we can't actually trade. So in order make back your "nut" (yes, it's also called that), you need to trade/ride beyond your theta.

And of course there is the vega variable. Theta assumes a constant volatility, but as we all know too well, volatility can move. Of course it can move in your favor. But it's a risk, and a difficult one to offset. And so on.

Greeks are the building blocks of the options world. But volatility is really the lifeblood. Let's say we now learn a thing or two about this CBOE Volatility Index, the VIX and the general concept of volatility.

# Chapter 3

# UNDERSTANDING
# THE VIX

In Chapter 2, we learned a thing or two about Greeks. We continue
on here with an introduction to volatility and the Craze of the
Aughts—the VIX.

Volatility comes in two basic stripes; historical and implied. Historical volatility (HV) is also called "realized" volatility. It refers to an
objectively calculated formula that measures the standard deviation
of an underlying instrument—in these pages generally a stock, ETF,
or index. It contains a specific number of days, all in the past. For
example, a 25-day HV of the Standard & Poor's 500 Index (SPX)
means we are seeing the volatility of the SPX itself over the past 25
trading days.

Implied volatility (IV) refers to the volatility implied by the price of
an option. The value of an option is calculated by a somewhat complex formula that includes several fixed variables such as price of the
underlying instrument, strike price of the option, time until expiration, dividends, and cost of carry, as well as a moving variable—the
volatility of the option. But if we know the price of the option, as we
do for everything that trades, we can then work backwards and calculate an implied volatility of that option.

How is an option priced? Well, it's a two-way auction market, just like stocks. An implied volatility represents the best guess of the "market" of the volatility of the underlying between now and when the option expires.

Options trade with all sorts of time until expiration. Volatility readings tend to normalize these numbers into fixed lengths. Far and away the most common implied volatility readings normalize into 30-day numbers. Unlike HV though, IV refers to calendar days. Hit up a screen on a web site like ivolatility.com and hit up a symbol, and dollars to donuts the first graph you see will show you 30-day implied and historical volatility for that symbol. Like the graph in Figure 3.1 for AMZN, covering a six-month period ending in early February 2009.

The lighter line represents the implied volatility of a normalized at-the-money option in AMZN with 30 days until expiration. Obviously we do not always have an option right at the money with that exact duration; generally, we have neither. So whoever is calculating the number uses a generally proprietary formula to create just such an option.

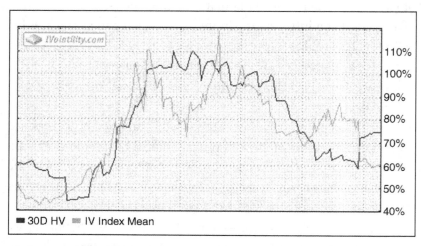

**Figure 3-1**  AMZN 30 Day IV and HV, August 2008–February 2009

The dark line represents 30-day historical volatility of AMZN stock. Remember that these two readings are not directly comparable, primarily because HV looks backwards at all times, and IV estimates forward. We advance that concept further in the next chapter. For now, we will discuss the most popular of all volatility measures, the VIX.

## ...And I Probably Had a Real Life Back Then Also

The time is 1993. Bill Clinton is inaugurated. The Buffalo Bills lose their third straight Super Bowl and run headstrong into a 4th. The World Wide Web begins. Nirvana releases "In Utero."

And the VIX was born.

The goal?

To provide a handy estimate of the implied volatility of a 30-day at-the-money option on the S&P 100 index, also known as the OEX.

The original VIX was the brainchild of Professor Robert E. Whaley of Duke University and was first revealed in a presentation to the Chicago Board Options Exchange (CBOE). We barely notice the OEX these days, but back in 1992, OEX accounted for roughly 75 percent of all index options volume and thus provided the logical choice for an underlying index.

Professor Whaley recalled those early days in a presentation at the Owen Graduate School of Management at Vanderbilt University, where he currently teaches.

> To begin, VIX is an index, like the Dow 30, computed on a real-time basis throughout each trading day. The only meaningful difference is that it measures volatility and not price. VIX was introduced in 1993 with two purposes in mind. First, it was intended to provide a benchmark of expected short-term market

volatility. To facilitate comparisons of the then-current VIX level with historical levels, minute-by-minute values were computed using index option prices dating back to the beginning of January 1986. This was particularly important since documenting the level of market anxiety during the worst stock market crash since the Great Depression—the October 1987 crash—would provide useful benchmark information in assessing the degree of market turbulence experienced subsequently. Second, VIX was intended to provide an index upon which futures and options contracts on volatility could be written. The social benefits of trading volatility have long been recognized.

. . . In attempting to understand VIX, it is important to emphasize that it is forward-looking, measuring volatility that the investors expect to see. It is not backward-looking, measuring volatility that has been recently realized, as some commentators sometimes suggest.

Conceptually, VIX is like a bond's yield to maturity. Yield to maturity is the discount rate that equates a bond's price to the present value of its promised payments. As such, a bond's yield is implied by its current price and represents the expected future return of the bond over its remaining life. In the same manner, VIX is implied by the current prices of S&P 500 index options and represents expected future market volatility over the next 30 calendar days.

For about a decade, the VIX served as the de facto measuring stick for volatility. The original VIX based its calculation on a weighted average of the implied volatility of eight near-the-money call and put options on the OEX. Why just eight? As Professor Whaley notes:

Of the available option series at the time, at-the-money options were by far the most actively traded. Options with exercise prices away from the current stock index level were less actively traded and frequently had stale price quotes and relatively wide bid/ask spreads. Including such quotes in the real-time computation of the VIX would reduce its timeliness and accuracy.

## The VIX Is Dead; Long Live the VIX

The VIX existed in its original form for a decade. But by 2003, much had changed. The S&P 500 supplanted the OEX as the most popular index. As per Professor Whaley, 12.7 SPX contracts now trade for every 1 contract in OEX. In addition, the nature of order flow morphed over the years such that At-The-Money and Out-of-The-Money puts became the vehicle of choice to play index options as investors used them more and more as a simple form of portfolio insurance.

And there still was no trading vehicle associated with the VIX. Or any volatility index for that matter, as by 2003, there was also the CBOE Nasdaq Volatility Index (VXN). VXN duplicated the VIX, but it measured volatility on the Nasdaq 100 index.

So on September 23, a new VIX was born that had a new underlying index, the SPX, and a completely new methodology.

## Ch-Ch-Ch-Changes on the Way

The VIX would still strive to express an implied volatility for a hypothetical option with 30 days until expiration and would still consider options from two expiration cycles. But, as per the CBOE, "The new VIX generally uses put and call options in the two nearest-term expiration months in order to bracket a 30-day calendar period. However, with 8 days left to expiration, the new VIX 'rolls' to the second and third contract months in order to minimize pricing anomalies that might occur close to expiration."

And anomalies there are. As an option gets close to expiration, the pricing becomes less a volatility consideration and more a simple price consideration. And a slight tweak in price can have an outsized difference in the volatility of an option so close to expiration. An option going from 20 to 30 cents may jump 10–20 points in volatility terms. It's not a true reflection of volatility expectations for anything but the shortest of time frames, and thus it makes perfect sense to roll such options out of the calculation.

Further, ". . .The time of the VIX calculation is assumed to be 8:30 a.m. (Chicago time). The new VIX calculation measures the time to expiration, T, in minutes rather than days in order to replicate the precision that is commonly used by professional option and volatility traders."

Another sensible change. A strict "days until expiration" calculation treats 8:30 a.m. CST the same as 2:30 p.m. Yet the reality is they are very different; 8:30 a.m. includes virtually an entire extra day of trading from 2:30 p.m. All things being equal, an option has more value at 8:30 than it does at 2:30.

It's not perfect, however. By 2:30, traders anticipate the overnight decay and tend to price options accordingly. This gives the illusion of cheapened volatility when it is simply the clock. That is not accounted for. And about those ATM options. The CBOE will now include them in the calculation. Many of them. How many? It's a different answer each time.

Before we start, we need to determine the appropriate ATM strikes. It's not so simple as looking on the board and seeing the price of the SPX. We need the forward price, essentially the implied price of the SPX on expiration day based on the interest rates and dividends paid by the components between now and then. But we just need it to determine the right strike, not the exact value, so the CBOE simplifies it and just looks for the strike price where the difference between the call and the put is the smallest. Since it uses two expiration cycles, the ATM strike may differ, and both are used. They are referred to as K0.

And then, as the CBOE white paper says:

> Sort all of the options in ascending order by strike price. Select call options that have strike prices greater than K0 and a nonzero bid price. After encountering two consecutive calls with a bid price of zero, do not select any other calls. Next, select put options that have strike prices less than K0 and a nonzero bid price. After encountering two consecutive puts with a bid price of zero, do not select any other puts. Select both the put and call with strike price K0. Then average the quoted bid-ask prices for each option.

On a normal day, there's not much exactly concern about which strikes go into the calculation. But as we'll see later in the book, it's a methodology that can beget some shenanigans associated with VIX futures and options expiration.

And finally, "The new VIX is not calculated from the Black-Scholes option pricing model; the calculation is independent of any model. The new VIX uses a newly developed formula to derive expected volatility by averaging the weighted prices of out-of-the-money puts and calls."

Not that big a deal to 99.9 percent of the population, but a huge boon for those with issues on the Black-Scholes model. (The primary issue most have with Black-Scholes is that it does not accord enough value for outliers, or "fat tails.")

For those married to the old methodology, the CBOE has their backs as it continues to calculate and disseminate the number to this day, under symbol "VXO."

## This New VIX—
## Much Ado about Nothing?

An important fact that needs noting in all this? The OEX and the SPX pretty much move together like peanut butter and chocolate.

As Dr. Whaley notes in his paper from November 2008:

> For all intents and purposes, the S&P 100 and S&P 500 index portfolios are perfect substitutes. Over the period January 1986 through October 2008, the mean daily returns of the S&P 100 and S&P 500 were nearly identical, 0.0263 percent and 0.0266 percent, respectively, and the standard deviations of S&P 100 daily returns was only slightly higher than the S&P 500 returns, 1.182 percent and 1.138 percent, respectively. The correlation between their daily returns was 0.9898. The near perfect correlation between the return series implies that, holding other factors constant, OEX and SPX options are equally effective from a risk management standpoint.

So while it certainly made sense to switch from the standpoint that the SPX became the better product, it did not actually change the behavior of the index all that much.

And now that we had a new methodology and new attention given to volatility, the floodgates veritably poured open. On one track, we have a growing family of volatility indices from which to track, from VXN (Nasdaq) to RVX (Russell) into commodities such as OVX (oil) and different time frames such as VXV, which tracks theoretical 90-day SPX options. Going forward, the CBOE could apply the VIX methodology to any product and create, say, an Apple (AAPL) volatility index or a GOOG volatility index.

On the second track, the CBOE added tradable volatility products to the mix in 2004—first futures on the VIX, followed by options on the VIX futures. We get into this in detail in Chapter 8, but the gist of a VIX future is similar to that of an SPX. It's a cash-settled "bet" on the level of the VIX on the date of the future expiration. Since the VIX is a statistic that estimates volatility 30 days forward, a VIX future is a bet on where the market will estimate said volatility on a specific future date. An option is a "bet" on the underlying future and requires the buyer/seller to estimate the volatility of a volatility estimate.

Again, we delve into this in extreme detail later in the book.

## So What's Wrong with the VIX?

What's wrong with the VIX? Well, there's really nothing wrong with it per se. It just has its limitations. The VIX is a terrific tool to pop on a trading screen to get a handy estimate of market volatility—and fear. And it's consistent. The same way I can hit up the Dow or the S&P and get a quick market gauge.

But it's just that, an estimate. It is important to remember that volatility existed long before Whaley created the VIX. Options have traded off floor forever in varying forms. They turned transparent in the mid-1970s upon being listed on the CBOE. So volatility, the price for option protection or insurance, did not begin in 1993. It just became easier for the layperson to see it.

The VIX is not gospel and is not precise to the penny. In fact the best way to view the VIX is perhaps as a bit of a trading envelope. A move within that envelope most often represents nothing all that significant.

Different factors can bump or nudge down the VIX number, including something so simple as tightening or loosening some SPX options quotes. Many of these factors do not address the fear or complacency in the market but are better described as "quirks" or noise. Let's run over a few.

## The Calendar Quirk

The VIX expresses the "market" estimate for SPX volatility over the next 30 calendar days. But not all calendar days are created equal. What if it's a Friday and its December 19th? Traders look at their calendars and see a weekend, followed by a holiday-shortened week of low volume and low volatility as the markets are closed for Christmas the next Wednesday; followed by the same drill all over again the next week as the markets close for New Years.

Throw it all in, and trading figures to be subnormally inactive until Monday, January 5, a full 17 days later. That's a big chunk of the 30 days forward for the VIX estimates.

No trader in his right mind is paying full fare for an option on December 20; he will effectively forward the date on his option valuation model somewhere a week or two ahead of time. For ease of this example, let's say he pretends it is December 30, 10 days ahead. In plain English, he is saying an option with 30 days until expiration really only has 20 days until expiration. Thus he will lower his bids and offers on everything.

In his mind, he maintains the same volatility estimate; he just reduces the life of the option. And it makes sense because the underlying instrument will not realize normal volatility for the foreseeable future.

But here's the rub. No volatility equation will factor this in. The VIX, or any other formula, takes all the fixed variables, such as strike, price of the underlying, interest rates, dividends, time until expiration, and the price of the option itself, and solves for the unknown variable, the implied volatility of the option. When you reduce one of the "fixed" variables, namely, the price of the option, you reduce the variable you are solving for, the volatility. But the point would be that it's the *time* you should be reducing, not the implied volatility.

Remember, the trader's estimate for volatility has not actually changed.

And neither the VIX nor any formula adjusts time. All days are created equal. So ergo the VIX, or any volatility calculation in this particular situation, will understate the real volatility in the marketplace.

To illustrate this point, consider this example. We want to price a 30-day ATM call in the SPDR S&P 500 ETF (SPY). The price of SPY is 80, so let's use that as a strike price. The trader uses a 60 volatility to price the option, but it's December 20, and he reduces the time until expiration from 30 days to 20 days.

Throw it into a valuation program, and it's worth $4.50. So that's where she prices it.

But now to see what the volatility calculators say, we must work backwards. They pick up all the info, including the $4.50 price of the option, but *not* the reduced time the trader is using. The machine says it's at 48.7 volatility. In other words, the machine perceives a big drop in market volatility. In actuality, the trader still anticipates a 60 volatility, just not for the next 10 days.

It's important to note that the volatility calculation of 48.7 is technically correct. But the stated purpose for a volatility indicator is to measure fear and complacency, and 48.7 understates real fear and overstates real complacency. It simply recognizes that no one does much of anything around the Christmas/New Year's stretch.

This is an extreme example, but this same dynamic occurs in a smaller way ahead of holiday-shortened weeks, weekends, and even simply near a close. The updated VIX formula does it's best to account for the time-of-day issue, but even with that, there's a still a 17.5-hour time gap of inactive trading between a non-Friday close and the next day's open, and traders generally lower bids ahead of the overnight.

## The Skew Quirk

The skew quirk refers to the fact that the SPX, as well as most market or sector ETFs and individual stocks, has a skew in their pricing that puts trades at a higher price than the mirror call. That is, a put with a 40 delta almost always trades at a higher volatility than a call with a 40 delta and the same expiration. And that principal holds true for most puts and calls on the board. Why is this important to the VIX?

Remember the VIX, or any volatility calculation, weights components proportionate to how close they are to the money. The closer to the money, the greater the impact on the volatility index. So what happens when the market, or a stock, declines? The index, or stock, now sits nearer to lower strikes. And those lower strikes carry a higher volatility. Therefore a move lower in and of itself will produce a higher volatility reading even if every single option on the board is priced at the same volatility as it was before.

Hard to visualize? Pretend you are a market maker or specialist and have a position in pretty much every series in SPX. Each series has a modestly different volatility. SPX now goes a bit lower, but you do not change the volatility in any individual series. No change whatsoever in fear or complacency. Yet a calculation seeking a broad measure of volatility thinks volatility moved higher for the simple reason that the higher volatility strike prices are now closer to the money.

Again the VIX here is correct; it just perceives an uptick in fear that did not really happen.

How does this work in real life?

Let's go back to the SPY and say we have four strikes—the December 70s, 75s, 80s, and 85s. And let's say that the skew is such that the 70s carry a 60 volatility, the 75s carry a 55 volatility, the 80s carry a 50 volatility, and the 85s carry a 45 volatility.

Now we'll say that the stock is right at 80. The VIX on the SPY would ignore the 80s and use the other series. And it would come up with something like a 51 volatility.

Suppose SPY now declines the next day to 75, but all the above options carry the same volatility as they did when SPY was at 80.

The 75s get ignored, but the 70s now get much greater weight, and the VIX calculation will produce a number closer to 54. That's a three-point jump in this example, without an actual option changing in volatility terms.

## The News Quirk

Often options premiums simply tick up in anticipation of a news event for which the timing is known but the magnitude and direction are unknown. Say an election or a (Federal Reserve Board) meeting, or in the case of an individual stock, an earnings announcement. This of course leads to an uptick in volatility indicators—and again, an entirely accurate one. But in order to assess true fear and complacency in the market, one has to look far beyond the number resulting from the headline because that will reflect fear about only one event.

This one is not such a big deal. The only quibble I would have with it is that the VIX seeks to measure fear over a longer time horizon, 30 days, and this suggests that a disproportionate component of that stat has nothing to do with 29 of those days.

But here's an interesting side note. The introduction of VIX futures allows us to filter out near-term noise like that. VIX futures snapshot the expected VIX reading on the day it expires and thus will not react much to very short-term noise.

Again, we get much more into VIX futures and options in Chapter 8.

## Summary

The past five years or so have seen an exponential increase in awareness of volatility. And the VIX serves as the standard bearer, and in fact the way most people define volatility. The indicator serves its purpose the same way as the Dow serves its purpose, namely as a one-stop shop where anyone can assess fear and complacency.

The VIX has flaws however, not in concept, or methodology, but rather in its inability to perfectly reflect the volatility landscape. But perhaps *flaw* is not the right word. It measures what it sets out to measure; it's just that volatility imperfectly measures fear at different times. In other words, VIX does not translate perfectly to the tick. And VIX analysis that relies too much on such precision is doomed to give a bevy of false signals. What can we do about this?

In the next chapter we get under the hood a bit further. Index volatility represents something of an equilibrium of sorts. But how do we get to that point? You are about to find out.

# Chapter 4

# NUTS AND BOLTS VIX

The VIX has some warts, as we saw in Chapter 2, but it certainly "works" up to its stated purpose. But you can't please all the people all of the time.

It's December 2008, and Bloomberg runs this: "VIX Fails to Forecast S&P 500 Drop, Loses Followers."

Investors are starting to abandon volatility as a forecasting tool for stocks after one of the most-used measures of price swings failed to anticipate the biggest monthly decline in U.S. equities in 21 years.

The Chicago Board Options Exchange Volatility Index flashed "buy" signals for the Standard & Poor's 500 Index during October's 17 percent drop, the biggest since the stock market crashed in 1987. The so-called VIX also lost 44 percent since Nov. 20, a bearish signal, even as the S&P 500 rose 18 percent.

Money managers relied on the 18-year-old VIX as a guide for the S&P 500 because the gauge correctly predicted the equity index's range 84 percent of the time and signaled the end of the bear market in 2002. Volatility, along with stock valuations and equity analysts, failed to signal the scope of declines in the worst year for stocks since 1931 as $1 trillion in credit losses spurred the first simultaneous recessions in the U.S., Europe and Japan since World War II.

"It used to be that an extreme one-week move in the VIX either up or down would give you predictive power, and now it's just completely broken down," said Stu Rosenthal, money manager at Volaris Volatility Management, a unit of Credit Suisse Group AG in New York that oversees $4 billion and handles volatility trading strategies for pension funds, hedge funds and wealthy individuals. "You have only 18 years of data, most of which was during one of the greatest bull markets in history."

Well, where to begin? It's kind of a faulty premise that the VIX predicts in the same manner that a point spread predicts how a football game will go. It's a guideline based on both past results and future expectations. But consider a football teaser. One teaser lets you move 4 point-spreads by 13 points each. But you must pick all four games correctly to win the bet. Assuming that bookies don't give money away on them, it implies that you have about an 84 percent chance to win each individual game. This in turn implies that 68 percent of games fall within 13 points above or below the point spread, which in turn implies that almost a third of all games finish what we'll call "about one standard deviation" away from the spread. So by the logic of the article, that renders point spreads utterly useless.

Common sense says that options won't always fairly price future events and will sometimes price very poorly. Volatility moves, baby! At times it moves quite swiftly.

What does implied volatility do? Well, it's essentially a customized measure of standard deviation. In the case of the VIX, a very simple formula can tell you the expected range in a day for the underlying instrument (SPX). Divide the VIX by the square root of 252 (the number of trading days per year), and you get a range within which SPX is expected to trade in a day. In other words, a VIX of 32 implies a roughly 2 percent range in the SPX in a given day.

But here's the point that Bloomberg's article misses. That's a probability, not a guarantee. Specifically, the SPX should stay within that range 68 percent of the time; that's it. A violation, frequent moves beyond 2 percent, does not make the VIX wrong. It's just more exception than rule.

Anyway, let's roll up those sleeves and see what the VIX actually does tell us.

## Divided We Stand; Together We Fall

At its core, index volatility has two components. One is the volatility of the underlying components. The other is the degree to which those components correlate with each another.

The former clearly has a positive correlation; the more volatile the "troops," the more volatile a measure that indexes those troops, such as the VIX.

The latter however is arguably even more important. If stocks, or major sectors, are moving violently, but in opposition, the net impact on an index that includes them is dampened volatility. Consider the time stretch from the beginning of 2007 to mid-year 2008. We had one gigantic market sector, energy, in full boom mode. (See Figure 4.1.)

While at the same time, another sector hit the skids, financials. (See Figure 4.2.)

All the while, the VIX lifted but from a historically low level, generally in the teens, to the rather mediocre low 20s. (See Figure 4.3.)

Many an article was penned in a futile effort to explain why a world where credit markets froze, financial giants went to the woodshed and beyond, and volatility of individual names in the financial space soared

**Figure 4-1**

**Figure 4-2**

**$VIX** (Volatility Index - New Methodology) INDX    © StockCharts.com
30-Jun-2008 4:00pm  **O** 24.25  **H** 24.26  **L** 23.27  **Last** 23.95  **Chg** +0.51 (+2.18%) ▲
$VIX (Daily) 23.95
MA(20) 22.22
MA(50) 20.21
MA(200) 22.74

**Figure 4-3**

to the moon, could the VIX stay so historically mediocre. But the answer was right in front of us. Don Fishback of Don Fishback's Market Update measured, weighted, and indexed implied volatility of S&P 500 component stocks (known proprietarily as ODDS SPXIV) and produced the graph shown in Figure 4.4, and the following explanation.

> Here's how I built the chart. First, the blue (darker) line is simply the one-month moving average of my ODDS SPXIV minus VIX. Its axis is shaded in the same blue color.
>
> The second line, the red (lighter) one, is a bit more complicated. It is the average of the one-year correlation of each of the Select SPDR Industry Groups compared to SPY. For instance, I calculated the one-year correlation of XLF compared to SPY. I then repeated the process for each of the Select SPDRs. I then took the average of each of these individual correlations. [Again,

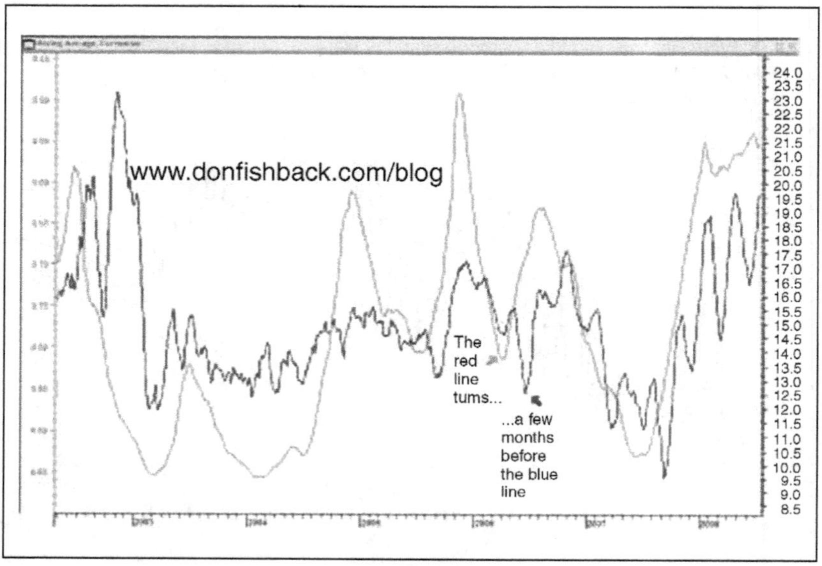

**Figure 4-4**

I realize it's not mathematically perfect. But we're simply looking for a simple explanation that can be perfected later.] When
I graphed the correlation line, I flipped its axis upside down (see
the red numbers in the y-axis to the left), so that the higher the
correlation, the further down the chart the indicator line fell.

Here's how to interpret the chart: When industry group correlation is high (red line low), most industry groups should be
moving in the same direction. If financials crater, materials,
energy and utilities should also be collapsing, so a broad-based
stock index like the S&P 500 should also be going down hard.
Everything moves together, so index volatility and individual
stock volatility should not diverge. The difference in VIX and
ODDS SPXIV should narrow. That means the blue line should
decline. As noted previously, because correlation's axis is flipped

upside down, rising correlation will appear as a decline in the red line. That means a low point in the red line should be associated with a low point in the blue line.

On the other hand, if correlation is declining (indicated by the red line rising), then the difference between VIX and ODDS SPXIV should expand (indicated by the blue line rising).

What's fascinating about this graph is when you look at the peaks and troughs of each line. The red line tends to peak before the blue line. That is, correlation tends to lead the volatility differential by about three months. That is, when you start to see correlation rise, a few weeks later you're likely to see the gap between the implied volatility of individual stock options and the implied volatility of index options narrow.

That's an important note that bears repeating. The blue line does NOT graph overall volatility. It measures the difference in the implied volatility of individual stock options versus index option volatility. Think of it as a dispersion measuring tool. When correlation is low, index options don't provide as much protection as you might think. Buying VIX calls, which has been touted as a hedging tool, will not provide much protection either.

In sum, in this seemingly neverending pursuit to explain why VIX isn't climbing as fast as many think it should given the magnitude of the stock market's decline, the reason VIX is stuck in the mid-20s can be explained by two factors: sector correlation is currently quite low, and the 10% decline off of the May peak took more than a month

Fast forward to the second half of 2008, and the answer became pretty clear to all. Energy and financial and pretty much everything else started moving in unison. And lower. And market volatility soared. Here's a chart of SPY 30-day implied (light) and historical (dark) volatility in the second half of 2008. (See Figure.4.5.)

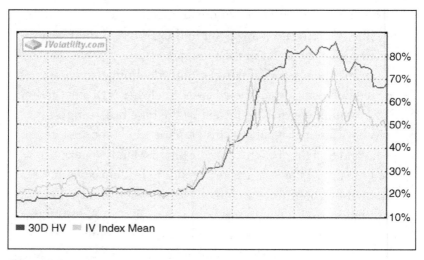

**Figure 4-5**

So now we know why the VIX does what it does. But it leaves many crucial questions.

## Can We Predict the VIX?

One crucial question is, Can we predict the VIX? The answer is, to some extent, yes.

Michael Stokes at MarketSci blog studies the question, and responds with this:

> For the most part, the absolute VIX level is a function of recent market volatility (not necessarily future volatility). As depicted in the graph below, there is an 84% correlation between the previous 20-day standard deviation (volatility) of S&P 500 returns and the absolute level of the VIX. Linear reg. equation for the chart above: Estimated Absolute Value (EAV) = 1244.0x + 7.7

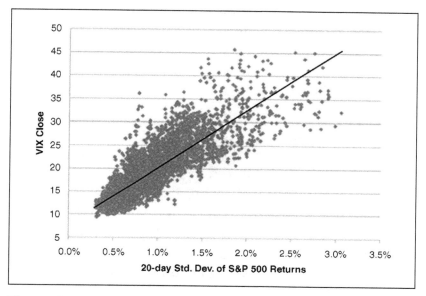

**Figure 4-6**

To a lesser degree, day-to-day changes on the VIX are a function of day-to-day changes on the S&P 500. As depicted in the second graph, there is a –69% correlation between (lognormal) changes in the two.

Linear reg. equation for the chart above: Estimated Price Change % (EPC) = –4.0x

Putting these two factors into a very SWAG'ish formula for predicting the VIX we get something like Estimated VIX = EAV + (EAV * EPC).

A graph of these estimated versus actual VIX values looks very tight.

That's an 85% correlation (r– squared = 72%). By comparison, that's about the same level of predictive ability the S&P 500

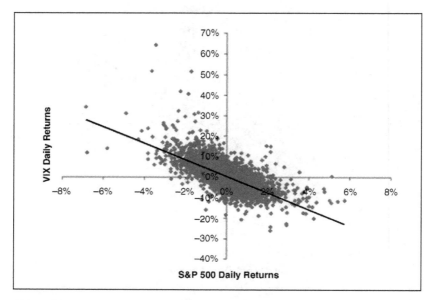

**Figure 4-7**

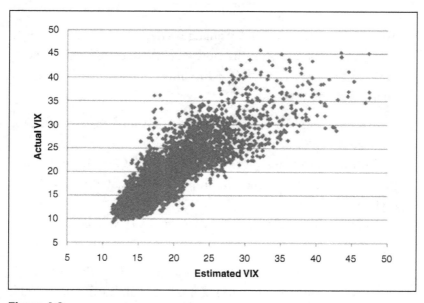

**Figure 4-8**

has in determining the value of the Nasdaq 100 (and that's pretty darn high).

Move out to 25 days, and the correlation is pretty much the same (.8484). As it is for 30 days (.8493).

But here's the interesting thing. Implied volatility ostensibly predicts future realized volatility in the underlying. On a given day, the historical reading tells you the volatility realized by the underlying over the past (x) days, whereas implied volatility predicts going forward, generally 30 days. So a better test involves offsetting the two. In other words, let's say we use 30-day readings for both. Implied volatility today covers the same time period as 30-day HV as read 30 days from today. Well, almost. HV counts only trading days; IV counts all calendar days. Ostensibly implied volatility should predict that 30-day HV pretty well (and really 25-day HV too).

And yes it does well, but not as well as above. 30-day HV in the VIX, offset 30 days into the future, has a .7434 correlation to the VIX. Notably, that's .10 below a concurrent VIX and 30-day HV reading.

So in other words, implied volatility does a better job of telling you something you already know (realized volatility over the past month or so) than it does predicting future volatility. And that's significant because *that's what IV sets out to do*—price and predict future volatility.

What does that spell? Modest inefficiency in the options market. Opportunity.

As a general rule, options overprice actual risk, at least in volatility terms. Options can spend months at a time trading at a higher volatility than a 30-day HV ever sees. Witness 2005 and 2006 as recent examples.

Figure 4.9 shows what IWM looked like in 2006.

Again, the lighter line represents implied volatility, and the darker line the 30-day volatility of the stock itself. If you squint, you can find

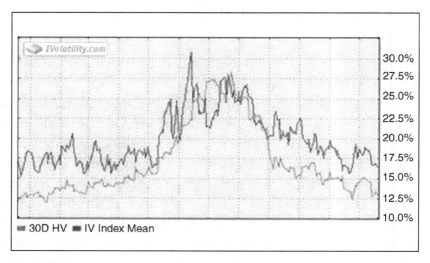

**Figure 4-9**

a few days around midyear where HV exceeded IV. And note also the low absolute numbers. Hard to believe, but an ETF that tracked the Russell spent roughly half the year under a 15 volatility. That translates into an expected range of about 1 percent per day.

And it wasn't just indices with this behavior. Figure 4.10 shows a chart of Google (GOOG) from 2006.

There are basically two blips above the IV, and both were literally blips, big one-day reactions to earnings reports, of which options were bid up ahead of time. So I would make the case that if you offset the HV to correspond to the IV (in other words, visually move the darker line one horizontal line to the left), GOOG spent an entire year trading less volatile than the options priced in.

But alas, we can't just blindly sell options. There's a reason they tend to overbid: tail risk. The possibility you walk in one day and a stock has moved 10, 20, 30 percent on some news item. A perpetual option seller can earn money for the better part of a year and then

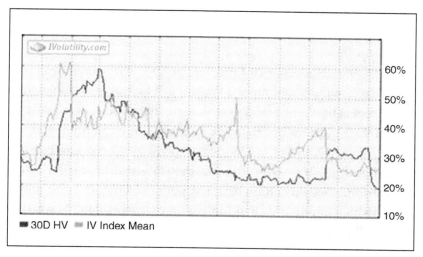

**Figure 4-10**

blow it all on one big gap against him. Or a monster one-way trend, like financial stock bashing in 2008. It's an outlier event, but by nature it's unpredictable in timing.

## Summary

What can the VIX do for you? It can tell you an expected range in the underlying index, the SPX. In fact any volatility measure will tell you the expected range in its underlying. Remember though that is a *probability*, not a guarantee. Otherwise, shorting every option with a strike a certain percentage above or below the current stock price would result in free money.

Market volatility expectations reside at the intersection of two factors: volatility of the component stocks and the degree to which they correlate. The volatility surge in mid-2008 had as much to do with increased correlation as anything else—specifically, energy imploding alongside everything else. Correlation does not happen in a vacuum, however, as it is a byproduct, in and of itself, of a more volatile backdrop.

As a general rule, we can predict the VIX with some impressive degree of accuracy very simply. We can just look at realized volatility in the recent past. The problem is, though, that there's not much value added there; it does not translate to predicting something you can trade, like a VIX future, or the market itself. What else can you predict about the VIX? Well, it has some statistical biases that cause overperformance on certain days and weeks and months, and underperformance in others. Is that something we can exploit? Maybe yes, but you'll have to turn the page to find out how.

# Chapter 5

# VOLATILITY TIMING

As we note in Chapters 3 and 4, we have some quirks in the VIX—and really in any volatility calculation. To some extent these quirks represent "noise." No volatility index can ever perfectly capture fear to the penny. Knowing that the VIX may rise or fall in a given day or week or month does not necessarily provide a tradable opportunity. But it might. So let's dig in.

First, let's examine day of the week bias. That is the tendency of options to cheapen ahead of a weekend as traders face three days of time decay and then recapture a bit on Monday. We classify this as "noise" in that it does not portray real fear of anything other than losing some premium on your holdings at a time when you can't flip stock against it for a few days.

Using data from January 1, 1990, to December 31, 2007, we calculate the average daily VIX change relative to the prior day's close. (See Table 5.1.)

Well, it's a pretty small tweak in every day but one, Monday. But that one is fairly significant. All things being perfectly equal, the VIX lifts by 2.3 percent on Mondays.

And again, we have a logical explanation. Traders lower bids and offers late Friday to account for the extra weekend decay. And Friday

**Table 5.1**   Average Change In VIX by Day of Week

| Day | Change |
| --- | --- |
| Monday | +2.301% |
| Tuesday | −0.1163% |
| Wednesday | −0.5254% |
| Thursday | +0.0957% |
| Friday | −0.713% |

is indeed the weakest day, although only one-third the magnitude of the Monday gain.

So why is this noise and not opportunity? Because it's a pretty widely known or assumed concept, and you have no tradable play on this knowledge. Buy some actual options ahead of the volatility pop you know will happen, and your gain in volatility terms merely offsets the loss of time decay over the weekend. In fact, that's exactly why it happens in the first place.

To illustrate, suppose you have a hypothetical option, XYZ. It's Friday, and you want to buy some ATM calls and you see that volatility has declined a few points, which translates into a 50-cent "discount." So you buy some. Then Monday rolls around, and volatility has increased back to where it was before the Friday sell-off. And the stock is unchanged. Yet the options are now 25 cents cheaper in actual dollars than when you bought them.

What in the world is going on? Must be those darned market makers hosing you somehow.

Well, not quite.

Let's say these XYZ calls have a .25 theta, meaning that each day they decline by 25 cents in value from the day before. All other things equal. So on late Friday, facing three days of decay, the traders start to anticipate the weekend and decide they could safely reduce their bids and offers to reflect that. They lowered it the equivalent of two of those days, because there is always the possibility of news, and a gap, before the next session. Well, that 50 cents translated to a few volatility points when viewed through the prism that the calendar still says it's Friday.

Fast forward to Monday, and volatility has returned to "normal." As has the calendar. The calls spike up in volatility, yet it's three days later, so the absolute price has actually declined by 25 cents.

So you say, what about trading a VIX product? Well if you had spot VIX an ETF that just tracked the actual VIX, you could buy it at Friday's close and sell it at Monday's open. That's precisely why we don't have one. The VIX is merely a statistic with vagaries like this.

And a future and the one-month ETN won't help you because traders know this dynamic and will price the VIX futures and, in turn, the VIX options, accordingly. Not enough data in the system yet to draw any meaningful conclusions, but I hereby predict that with a decade of data, we will find that Friday futures prices will become the fattest relative to the VIX itself.

## Where You Sit May Depend on When You Sit

Options order flow has a rhyme and reason to it. Buy writes represent the most common play, so call selling dominates order flow in the general sense. But what happens when that written call expires? Sometimes it's in the money, and the customer just takes the options assignment as a way to sell the stock. Other times though the seller rolls to a different and further month.

Most rolling takes place on or near expiration. In fact The CBOE S&P 500 BuyWrite Index (BXM) (see Chapter 7), rolls on expiration, as would any fund seeking to track its performance. So if that's the case, one might expect a slight nudge down in volatility just before or just after expiration.

Does it happen, though?

Table 5.2 shows the average VIX reading at the close of each day in the expiration cycle. For the purposes of this and other tables, we label every day in every expiration cycle from Day 1 (expiration day)

**Table 5.2**   VIX by Day in Expiration Cycle

| Day of Cycle | Average VIX | Median VIX |
|---|---|---|
| Day 22 | 17.78 | 16.14 |
| Day 25 | 17.9386 | 17.265 |
| Day 23 | 18.0476 | 16.92 |
| Day 24 | 18.1419 | 16.93 |
| Day 21 | 18.2029 | 16.775 |
| Day 1 | 18.5433 | 17.13 |
| Day 2 | 18.6650 | 17.225 |
| Day 18 | 18.7295 | 17.18 |
| Day 16 | 18.7694 | 17.29 |
| Day 17 | 18.8098 | 17.14 |
| Day 3 | 18.8832 | 17.745 |
| Day 11 | 18.9367 | 17.63 |
| Day 19 | 18.9466 | 17.385 |
| Day 13 | 19.0026 | 17.90 |
| Day 4 | 19.0221 | 17.99 |
| Day 12 | 19.1144 | 18.01 |
| Day 15 | 19.1509 | 17.84 |
| Day 6 | 19.1565 | 18.12 |
| Day 14 | 19.1900 | 18.24 |
| Day 20 | 19.2127 | 17.35 |
| Day 8 | 19.2978 | 18.14 |
| Day 9 | 19.3203 | 18.13 |
| Day 7 | 19.3586 | 18.35 |
| Day 5 | 19.3730 | 18.07 |
| Day 10 | 19.7120 | 18.72 |

to Day 25 (the first Monday after expiration in a five-week cycle). Note that some expiration cycles contain four weeks and some contain five weeks, so about two-thirds of the time, the cycle ends at Day 20.

We then ranked each day by the average VIX close. Additionally we include medians, primarily to spot outliers.

There is a major tendency toward low readings early in the five-week cycle. In fact the five lowest average VIX readings occur on Days 21 to 25, reinforcing my anecdotal impression that Week 1 of a five-week cycle represents the single worst time to own an option.

Day 1 (expiration day) and Day 2 take up the next two spots on the volatility wall of shame.

Using medians tells a similar story, albeit with a couple variations on both ends of the spectrum.

So here's a word to the wise. If you intend to buy options, avoid the very end of an expiration cycle and the beginning of the next one.

And what is the best time to own options, at least in terms of your prospects for having options volatility hold up? Pretty clearly the next to last week in the cycle. Four of the best five days occur then.

But wait. What if we adjust each day in the cycle for the day of the week it falls on? For example, Day 5 always falls on a Monday, Day 4 always falls on a Tuesday, and so on, so let's use Table 5.2 as a multiplier and rerank the days in the month. (See Table 5.3.)

It's pretty clear that we have a pattern and a preliminary trading thought here. If you have a mind to short options, be it to roll calls as part of a buy-write or whatever, don't wait until expiration day. In fact Day 6, the Friday a week before expiration, looks ideal on the surface as you get your options sale off right before implied volatility typically hits a trough.

On the flip side, if you are of a mind to buy options, it looks like you want to get in about Day 15 or so, the Monday three weeks ahead of expiration.

**Table 5.3** Adjusted VIX By Day in Expiration Cycle

| Day | Average Volatility, Adjusted |
| --- | --- |
| Day 25 | 17.5351 |
| Day 22 | 17.7630 |
| Day 23 | 18.1429 |
| Day 24 | 18.1630 |
| Day 21 | 18.3336 |
| Day 2 | 18.6472 |
| Day 1 | 18.6472 |
| Day 15 | 18.7201 |
| Day 20 | 18.7805 |
| Day 17 | 18.7918 |
| Day 18 | 18.8285 |
| Day 16 | 18.9042 |
| Day 5 | 18.9372 |
| Day 19 | 18.9687 |
| Day 3 | 18.9830 |
| Day 4 | 19.0442 |
| Day 11 | 19.0727 |
| Day 12 | 19.0961 |
| Day 13 | 19.1029 |
| Day 14 | 19.2124 |
| Day 10 | 19.2686 |
| Day 6 | 19.2940 |
| Day 7 | 19.3400 |
| Day 9 | 19.3428 |
| Day 8 | 19.3998 |

But wait again, this still does not tell the complete story. There are two other key factors in play here before we sign off on this time of the month concept.

Do the ebbs and flows of implied volatility simply correspond to ebbs and flows in realized volatility? Remember, always, in the general sense that an option purchase works when you pay a lower volatility than the stock trades at between now and when the option expires.

And the answer is? Not really.

We calculated five-day HVs for each day of the cycle and then correlated them back to the VIX. Offset by five days since the HV looks backwards. In other words, Day 6 on our system above (the Friday before expiration) would correspond to the five-day HV looking backwards from Day 1 (expiration day).

Correlation by this method was .01. So, not much relationship.

The other consideration is that options do not decay in a straight line. The closer to expiration, the faster the time decay. So it's all fine and good to own options that have the wind at their back in volatility terms, as looks like the case for options with roughly three trading weeks until expiration. But in the real world, we need to know how that translates into actual prices.

To illustrate the point, I created a hypothetical near-the-money SPX option. I used a strike of 900 with a price of 895 in SPX, with volatility of 20. And I then assumed that neither SPX nor volatility budges for an entire five-week cycle so as to isolate the daily decay. Table 5.4 shows the theoretical value of the call heading into each day.

Or if you prefer, Figure 5.1 shows the same information in chart form.

As you can see in the figure, while buying options on, say, Day 15 might make sense in volatility terms, it very much might cause problems in real terms as the decay in a near-month option will more than offset the volatility edge.

But here's the important point. You don't have to buy a near-month option. What if you bought the second cycle out? You suffer relatively minimal time decay. Say you buy this very same SPX option on the

**Table 5.4**   Value of SPX Option By Day of Cycle

| | |
|---|---|
| Day 25 | 18.08 |
| Day 24 | 17.78 |
| Day 23 | 17.47 |
| Day 22 | 17.16 |
| Day 21 | 16.85 |
| Day 20 | 15.89 |
| Day 19 | 15.55 |
| Day 18 | 15.2 |
| Day 17 | 14.86 |
| Day 16 | 14.5 |
| Day 15 | 13.38 |
| Day 14 | 12.96 |
| Day 13 | 12.55 |
| Day 12 | 12.13 |
| Day 11 | 11.69 |
| Day 10 | 10.27 |
| Day 9 | 9.76 |
| Day 8 | 9.22 |
| Day 7 | 8.65 |
| Day 6 | 8.05 |
| Day 5 | 5.97 |
| Day 4 | 5.15 |
| Day 3 | 4.22 |
| Day 2 | 3.12 |
| Day 1 | 1.75 |

Monday one cycle earlier, with eight full trading weeks to go until it expires. Then you hold it for two full trading weeks and sell it on the Friday pre-expiration. You will pay about $23.66 and then be able to sell it for $20.89, a relatively minimal amount of decay vs. the $6.33 it would cost you to hold that option in the near month (Days 19 to 8).

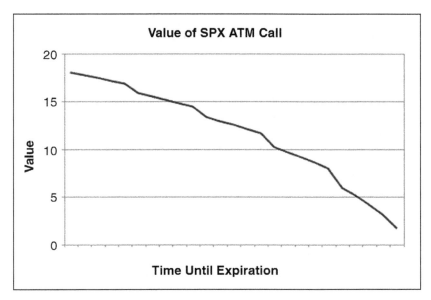

Value of SPX ATM Call

**Figure 5-1**

What do you get for that $2.77 ($23.66 – 20.89)? Not a lot, and that's the problem.

An option gives you gamma, the degree to which the delta of an option changes per 1 point move in the underlying. (See Chapter 2: Know Your Greeks, for a fuller explanation.)

This particular option in question, with eight weeks to go, has an average gamma of .0061 over the two-week holding time vs. .0123 if we held that same option in the near month. That's half as much gamma, meaning half as much ammo to fade moves in SPX.

Look at it this way: Instead of owning a call, say we own a straddle. Or to better illustrate, 10 straddles. The straddle is "delta neutral" at the time of purchase. If we buy the second month out, that gives us a positional gamma of .061 x 2 (it's a straddle, so we have to double it), meaning that for every point up in SPX, we get longer by 12 shares

(.061 x 2 x 100). So if SPX rallies by 8 points or so, we now have the ammunition to sell 100 shares and stay flat. If it rallies roughly another 8 points, we can sell another 100 shares. And so on. Conversely, in dips, we can buy back.

The nearer-month shares have about two times the gamma, so thus we have the ammo to fade stock on a four-point move.

Sounds great, but remember we're paying over twice as much for that right.

That's precisely the trade-off. And it's a subjective judgment. More gamma versus more decay. If you have a mind to own options, you get a similar bang for your buck going out in time when you factor in the lost gamma.

So what can we say about buying options? Well, to get a small volatility advantage, buy them with about three weeks left in the expiration cycle. And pick your cycle based on your overall volatility expectations. If you expect it in the here and now, go with the near month; if not, go out in time.

## How about the Sell Side?

Well clearly we have the inverse argument going on with the sell side. We have the wind at our back to begin with in the form of daily options decay. But we sure want to avoid shorting options ahead of a volatility lift.

It's pretty clear in volatility terms that sales make the most sense just ahead of the buy-write rolling pack. If the pack is doing it right before and right after expiration day one cycle ahead of the month you want to sell, there is no better time than right before that, sometime like Monday or Tuesday of expiration week. Days 3, 4, and 5 of the expiration cycle (Monday, Tuesday, and Wednesday) all carry midrange average volatilities.

The daily decay you earn at first is mediocre, but so is the gamma you risk—about .007 using the same SPX option as above.

So now we have settled on days we want to concentrate buying and selling and you're wondering, "Are there any monthly biases?"

Glad you asked.

Using data from January 1, 1990, to December 31, 2007, Table 5.5 shows the average and median VIX reading in each cycle month. Keep in mind that these are not quite calendar months because the cycle ends on the third Friday.

The results shown in the table are not that surprising. If you have ever stood in a pit in the summer, you would probably surmise that staring at the screens indoors while golf and tennis and the beach beckon did not exactly do you a favor. If you own options, you can get an occasional outlier event, like the July 2002 meltdown, the Asian contagion, or the Russian tea room (or whatever they called the Russian collapse in 1998). But by and large summer trades slowly.

**Table 5.5** VIX By Expiration Cycle

| Month | Average VIX | Median VIX |
| --- | --- | --- |
| January | 18.4464 | 18.19 |
| February | 18.8280 | 18.51 |
| March | 18.9750 | 18.68 |
| April | 18.5841 | 17.77 |
| May | 18.1117 | 17.195 |
| June | 17.7418 | 17.215 |
| July | 17.3124 | 16.705 |
| August | 18.9963 | 17.94 |
| September | 20.4407 | 17.995 |
| October | 20.6260 | 17.45 |
| November | 20.3808 | 17.29 |
| December | 19.1489 | 19.72 |

Likewise, it would hardly shock a soul to see that the September/October/November stretch, better known by 99.9 percent of the population as "autumn," provides the highest volatility of the year. Comparing that to the median though provides a bit of intrigue. Median fall VIX actually looks oddly mediocre, which says that in that 18-year time frame, a typical fall day looked like any other, minus the foliage. But if an outlier, fat tail, or whatever you want to call it, should strike, look out above.

This is all just implied volatility. We must compare it to realized volatility to assess the merits of options ownership. To accomplish this, we will calculate a 25- (trading) day HV for each month, offset it one month out, and compare it to the IV above. All this is expressed as a ratio. The higher the ratio, the higher IV we would typically pay relative to the HV we actually realize. And hence the less attractive it is to net buy options. (See Table 5.6.)

**Table 5.6** Implied vs. Realized Volatility Ratio by Month

| IV Month | Average IV/HV Ratio | Median IV/Average HV | Median IV/Median HV |
|---|---|---|---|
| January | 1.3771 | 1.3580 | 1.5006 |
| February | 1.3672 | 1.3441 | 1.4688 |
| March | 1.3022 | 1.2820 | 1.4319 |
| April | 1.2956 | 1.2388 | 1.3500 |
| May | 1.3560 | 1.2911 | 1.4292 |
| June | 1.3457 | 1.3058 | 1.3213 |
| July | 1.2522 | 1.2083 | 1.2433 |
| August | 1.2658 | 1.1955 | 1.4054 |
| September | 1.4200 | 1.2502 | 1.6102 |
| October | 1.2943 | 1.0956 | 1.4079 |
| November | 1.4843 | 1.2592 | 1.3085 |
| December | 1.5385 | 1.5843 | 1.6624 |

So basically owning cheap July volatility actually works—to some extent. Standing in a trading crowd, you generally get saddled with net long summer options. Closing your eyes and buying them into the morass tends to pan out though, at least relative to other times of the year. August works a bit too, though the numbers suggest that this has more to do with a couple outliers we mentioned. In addition, 9/11 throws off the August realized volatility as a 30-day option owned toward the end of the August 2001 cycle ultimately saw a realized volatility explosion. I don't like throwing numbers out in general because it becomes a slippery road of what to include and what not to include, so I'm just making a note of it.

And of course October—the king of all outliers. On a strictly median basis, it's not an especially good cycle to own. But this is more than offset by the occasional home run as well as the fact that traders take October volatility bursts pretty seriously and will also bid up options on any hint of action. And, as we'll see in a sec, better get there early in the cycle.

Noteworthy the other way? December stands out. And this makes intuitive sense. Volatility almost always increases during the fall, but actual stock movement bears that out. And by the time December rolls around (and remember that the December cycle rolls around near Thanksgiving), the music stops and the options are slow to catch on.

## For Our Next Trick, What If We Saw a Month in Half?

We have gone from the specific (daily volatility trends) to the general (monthly trends). Let's say that we combine the two. Let's divide each month into two halves—but not exactly halves. In four-week expiration cycles, we'll call Days 11–20 the first half, but in five-week cycles, we'll call Days 11–25 the first half. I understand that this is not exactly half, but experience says that the first couple of weeks tend to mesh as one in the elongated cycle. They act similarly.

Anyway, Table 5.7 shows the average VIX reading in the first "half" and second "half" of each monthly cycle over the same January 1, 1990, to December 31, 2007, time frame.

For most months, we see a pretty negligible variation.

Notable risers from the first to the second half include those we can explain by the calendar, such as January and July. Both have early to middle holiday breaks and thus see a bit of an options bid lowering ahead of the anticipated sluggish trade followed by a lift into normalcy later in the cycle. October we know tends to see an upswing in volatility in general. So August stands out as the oddball because there's no holiday affecting the trade on the front end, while the back end should

**Table 5.7**  Implied Volatility by Half-Cycle

| Month | First Half Mean | Second Half Mean | First Half Median | Second Half Median |
|-------|-----------------|------------------|-------------------|--------------------|
| January | 17.8419 | 19.0855 | 16.94 | 19.23 |
| February | 18.9247 | 18.7073 | 18.47 | 18.56 |
| March | 18.9874 | 18.9521 | 18.615 | 18.7 |
| April | 18.6794 | 18.4696 | 17.785 | 17.74 |
| May | 18.0317 | 18.2025 | 16.82 | 17.705 |
| June | 17.6777 | 17.8124 | 17.03 | 17.4 |
| July | 17.0357 | 17.6239 | 16.18 | 17.39 |
| August | 18.4218 | 19.6823 | 17.75 | 17.96 |
| September | 20.1976 | 20.7513 | 18.015 | 17.995 |
| October | 19.9820 | 21.3597 | 16.66 | 18.16 |
| November | 20.5982 | 20.121 | 17.04 | 17.455 |
| December | 19.4346 | 18.7983 | 20.09 | 18.81 |

start anticipating Labor Day and actually dip a smidge. But again, August has some outliers, so perhaps the median gives a truer picture. And that shows a whole lotta nothing.

Notable dippers? Remember from earlier in the chapter that volatility tends to peak in the next to last week of the cycle, so any dip would raise some eyebrows.

And it's really just December. And that has an easy explanation as the holiday season approaches.

## Summary

We've gone over many options tendencies, so how about we do some consolidation?

We're not going over the merits of net buying or net selling in any great detail in this chapter. We're just saying that when you maybe want to time trades *if* you buy or *if* you sell.

And in general, the trends suggest buying with about three weeks to go until expiration. Near month costs more in terms of the instant decay you face but benefits more in the added gamma you acquire. A slight up tick in realized volatility in the underlying results in a nice win on that trade, although we find no statistical evidence that suggests that you are a favorite to see that up tick.

As to selling, you get the best bang for your buck by selling the next month out about one week or so prior to expiration. In other words, sell Febs about a week ahead of January expiration, sell March a week ahead of Feb, and so on.

But don't enter either idea blind. July and October stand out as cycles you want to pounce a little earlier on any volatility dips as they tend to provide both good value relative to realized volatility and tendencies in January and October to see sustained volatility strength later in the cycle.

On the flip side, December options tend to start their near-month cycle with "fall pricing" before offering deals similar to those Christmas shoppers get. Sell early.

These are all just general trends. At the end of the day though, it's about one specific moment. What you paid or what you sold for, versus the stock and/or options action after you put on the trade. You still need to manage the position. Next up, we go into the mind of the active trader and see just that.

# Chapter 6

# HOW DO TRADERS TRADE VOLATILITY?

When last we met, we learned a bit about some tendencies of different parts of the expiration cycle. That's fine for helping pick spots on the margins, but the real money gets made managing positions you have on. At their core, trades come in two broad stripes— long and short volatility. The same position can flip from one side to the other on simply a move in the stock. But let's keep it simple for now and gaze into the minds of two traders, Long Gamma Man and Ms. Premium Seller.

## Buy High, Sell Low?

If you are being chased by a bear (the animal, not a market opinion), what is the key to getting away?

An old adage says that you don't have to actually outrun the bear, you simply have to outrun at least one person who's with you.

OK, bad joke. But we have an analogy here to pricing and trading options volatility.

You don't have to actually buy objectively cheap options and sell objectively fat options to make money. You can buy objectively fat options if you buy them cheap relative to the realized volatility between now and when the options expire.

Volatility in the S&P 500 averages about 20 over the course of history. But let's say you buy a one-month option at a 40 volatility. If realized volatility over the course of the month exceeds 40, you likely made money on the trade. Or at the very least you made a wise decision owning options instead of stock.

But that's just a generalization. It's truly not anywhere near that simple. In certain circumstances both a buyer and seller of volatility can make money, even if they had the exact opposite trade on. They can also both lose money.

So how about we get into some specifics—how actual option traders might look at both sides of the gamma coin.

## Everybody into the Water

Volatility serves as a proxy for the amount of money available in the options pool. Certainly in terms of opportunity, the deeper the pool (the greater the premiums), then the greater the opportunity for both buyers and sellers. For sellers, that's an obvious point. I mean of course the better the price they receive and the wider the range of stock with which they can profit. And the better compensation for assuming the risk of an outlier move in the stock.

For buyers, too, volatility spells opportunity. All they care about, or should care about, is whether the realized volatility of the stock itself will prove higher than the volatility they paid. And the beauty is that both sides can be right. Or wrong.

Let's consider one simple options trade, a straddle in First Solar (FSLR), one of the more consistently volatile stocks around. We will use a strike of $150 and a volatility of 80 and say that we have 30 days until expiration. Let's say Long Gamma Man buys 10 straddles from Ms. Premium Seller. The cost? Roughly $27.

Now we will do some fuzzy math on a couple of things here. An 80 volatility implies that the average day will see a 5 percent move (80/SQRT of 252). Well, actually, it implies that two-thirds of the days will see moves under 5 percent and that one-third will see moves above and beyond that. Now let's assume the implied volatility has fairly priced the ultimate realized volatility, so both Long Gamma Man and Ms. Premium Seller have equal opportunity to win on this trade.

Each trader has to now decide how he and she will manage the position. Long Gamma Man gets longer and longer FSLR as the stock rallies, and shorter and shorter as it declines. So he can fade into moves, but he must decide how aggressively.

Should he trade intra day to keep his delta flat?

Yes, he expects a range day, a session where we chop around and make little ground.

Should he simply wait until near the bell and just flatten his delta all at once?

Yes, if he expects a trend "low and last" or "high and last" sort of day.

Should he simply not do anything and shoot for longer-term trends?

Yes, if he feels we are in a longer-term trend.

How about Ms. Premium Seller? How should she handle her position, one with the diametrically opposite risks and rewards?

She will probably ignore the intraday swings. Overly aggressive trading is the best path to a losing play from her standpoint. If she is willing to sell premium, she must have the ability to withstand some chop. She ultimately has the wind at her back in the form of daily options decay. But should she hedge at the end of each day, flatten out?

Yes, if she suspects that she has gotten a high enough volatility to compensate for daily moves but is worried that a series of relatively small daily moves will ultimately add up into one bigger directional move.

Should she simply let nature take it's course and do nothing?

Well, she got $27 for the FSLR straddle, which means that if she sits tight and does absolutely nothing, she will profit if FSLR expires anywhere between $123 and $177 (that's the strike price plus or minus the premium she got for the straddle).

So as you can see, after the initial act of trading the straddle, we have so many variables that we can see any combo of results.

What do you say we get further into the minds of each side of the trade?

## Long Gamma Man

Simply put, Long Gamma Man might as well turn over an hourglass when he puts the position on. If we use the above example, he pays $27 for a straddle in FSLR that has an intrinsic value of 0. He has to figure out a way to make back that $27 before every last grain runs to the bottom of the glass, that is, expiration day.

How will he do this? The easiest way is to wake up one morning and find out that Germany will replace its entire energy complex with Mr. Sun. And FSLR simply gaps up to $200 or $250 or whatever. Or conversely, we find out that solar energy causes some newly discovered disease, and FSLR stock implodes.

Those are extreme examples and low probability events to say the least. If there is any inkling that a stock may have an overnight blast, the options probably reflect this to a great extent. Consider small cap biotechs for example. They tend to do little for most of the time. Then they double or halve overnight on FDA announcements. Options price accordingly.

What we do see in a stock like FSLR is gaps of the $10 or $15 or $20 variety. Long Gamma Man can pretty much expect that he will see one or two of them over the course of the month. That will produce a nice day when it happens, but what about the other 21 or 22 trading days? Long Gamma Man has the hourglass/time decay working against him. In his favor he has that long gamma position that gets him longer into strength and shorter into weakness. Therefore he can buy (fade) dips in the stock and then hope to sell it back out into strength. Or vice versa.

But he must make a decision. How aggressively should he fade moves? Remember from above that the volatility in FSLR trades at about an 80, meaning that FSLR needs to move 5 percent or so per day to pay for them. That 5 percent need not be "in a row" for his purposes. What if within a day, FSLR moves up and back within a 2 percent band or so. And it does it 10 different times. If he buys and sells over and over again, he can effectively capture a 20 percent move in one day. Providing of course that he knows that the range holds. Which of course he does not.

What if FSLR rallies by 2 percent, and he sells everything he can at that level, and then FSLR rallies another 2 percent? His gamma gets him long again, and he can sell again, but he has now locked in a mediocre average price on the day. He should be patient, especially if he repeats this trick a few more times.

What am I getting at? Long Gamma Man essentially has two choices each day. Trade aggressively and "flip off" that daily decay, or sit and wait and then buy or sell what he can at the close. He can even go a step further in that direction and let the moves of a few days accumulate before taking action.

Trading days do tend to come in one of the two varieties we noted above—trend days and range days. *Trend days* we loosely define as days when the stock, or the market as a whole, ends up somewhere close to high and last or low and last. Unless that action was incredibly volatile just getting to that close, the best course for Long Gamma Man is likely the golf course. Play 18 holes, get back to the machine at 3 p.m. Eastern time, and start hedging.

*Range days* are days when the market flops and chops and moves up and down within something resembling a range. Long Gamma Man would not want to miss a minute of this as the only way he could make back his daily decay is to flip, flip, flip, and flip some more.

Of course there's a catch. Long Gamma Man does not know whether he faces a trend day or a range day. So he'd better not get that tee time too early. No one knows. Pundits on TV would pretend they know, but in the real world, we can't divine the future. And that poses a problem for options owners. Long Gamma Man has the wind in his face, so to speak. He *has* to make good decisions on balance. The clock ticks, and his holdings decay. He'd better manage his position well.

Anecdotally, volatility tends to beget more volatility. And to the extent that trend days are a function of increased volatility, they tend to cluster. So my experience says that if you have a series of mostly trend days in the recent past, it pays to treat the day in front of you as a trend day too. This doesn't mean that you should literally go to the golf course and ignore what's happening, but it does mean that it makes sense to underhedge until the last hour or so.

Realistically, if I find myself sitting with Long Gamma Man's position, I will buy or sell *something* into all moves, even if I suspect a true trend day. I just would avoid flattening out too early and would also aggressively bid back for what I sold into strength. Or conversely, offer out what I bought into weakness.

Using the FSLR example, let's say that my gamma lets me short 500 shares up 10 points. But I suspect that FSLR keeps chugging ahead. I probably short 100 or 200 and then bid for it back somewhere.

Heads (the stock keeps rallying) I win; I am still long 300 or 400 and getting longer thanks to my positive gamma. Tails (it sells off) I buy back the 100 or 200 shares I sold. Obviously I misread the move for now, but at least I made a winning trade-off and salvaged something.

Conversely, a tough and rangy volatility environment tends to feed upon itself. In fact as a floor trader, I almost found the whole thing self-fulfilling. Big order sells options gamma to the trading crowd. Trading crowd now trades underlying stock very tightly, on the margins adding to any actual stock volatility decline. Upstairs desk sees cratering stock volatility and sells more options to the crowd. With options volatility now lower, crowd can trade ever tighter, pushing stock volatility even lower on the margins.

Rinse and repeat.

Now you throw all this in, and net owning options sounds like a lousy game. I mean you have to be right with some regularity to win. Who can guarantee that in what is effectively a zero sum game? No one.

But here's the kicker. You don't have to be right more than you are wrong per se. The risk/reward structure is asymmetrical. The risks tend toward the small dribblings out of decay day after day. The rewards tend toward the "wake up and find the stock gapping large" variety. It's almost like the thought process behind Texas hold 'em. You can withstand a series of small losses if you can max out those hands where you get dealt a pair of bullets.

In options speak, if Long Gamma Man can simply come close to even each mediocre day, he puts himself in prime position to get that occasional nice win when news hits. He can even lose modestly most days and come out okay. He doesn't know when the payday will come, much like poker players don't know when they will get a good hand to play. But Long Gamma Man does know that he can outlast the mediocre days. Or that at least should be his goal going in.

## Ms. Premium Seller

How many times have we heard the wisdom of net selling options? 70 percent go worthless? Too conservative! 80 percent go worthless? Seems like conventional wisdom. 90 percent go worthless? I have seen that number floated around too.

Seems like an easy game then. Sell options, hold your breath, win 70, 80, 90 percent of the time.

First of all, it's a myth. Those numbers generally refer to options still open on expiration day. In fact, according to the CBOE itself, 10 percent of options get exercised (and are thus clearly in the money) and 50–60 percent are closed out before expiration. We're talking about only 30–40 percent of outstanding options to begin with. So it's pretty much a case of selection bias. The options still remaining on the books are often still remaining on the books because they have no bid.

So it's safe to say that most options transacted actually do close with some value, whether they get exercised or closed via trade. This makes it sound like I argue against Ms. Premium Seller and net options shorting. I do not, because this does not tell the whole story either. An option does not have to close worthless for it to be a good sale. You can sell it and buy it back cheaper. Or sell it and get assigned but have it intrinsically worth less. And so on.

However you slice it, Ms. Premium Seller has the wind at her back. Time marches on and works in her favor. All things being equal, I like Ms. Seller's side of the trade better than Long Gamma Man's.

She has the opposite goal of Long Gamma Man. She does not have to call each day correctly. In fact, she can (and really should) trade poorly. She has to occasionally chase strength and short weakness. She has to defend a position that gets her shorter into rallies and longer into dips.

But again, she gets paid to do that. She is effectively the insurance company writing "policies." But unfortunately for her, policyholders sometimes make claims that she must make good on. If those claims come at a slow pace, she can effectively hedge and still come out whole or ahead. But what if her options shorts gap overnight? What if volatility explodes and she gets whipsawed chasing strength and fading weakness too many times?

Remember, her risks are asymmetric to the risks of the option longs. Long Gamma Man can lose only what he paid for his gamma, the actual options premiums. It tends to happen slowly. Ms. Premium Seller, however, has open, unlimited exposure. She is more likely to win in general, and certainly on a day-to-day basis. But her losses require a certain urgency to protect capital that option longs will almost necessarily never have.

And not to go all conspiracy theory here, but this dynamic is hardly a secret. Short premium is especially toxic around expiration. In fact, over the years, we have seen a coincidental policy change or two timed almost to the most vulnerable minute of the expiration cycle. I penned the following on my web site, DailyOptionsReport.com in response to one such moment on August expiration of 2007:

> So how does putting a market-moving Fed action as close to expiration as humanly possible have the maximal turbo effect? One word: Gamma.
>
> Consider a world where there is just one option, ATM SPY calls. They have a 50 delta, so let's say there is an open interest of 100 where each call gives you the right to buy 100 SPY's. If they are ATM, the calls have approximately a 50 delta, so presumably the call shorts own 5000 SPY's, while the longs are short the SPY's.
>
> But the delta changes as the stock moves. That's the gamma. Let's say the gamma is 10, so in other words if SPY lifts a point, the calls now have a 60 delta. The longs can thus sell 1000 SPY's up a point, while the shorts have to buy 1000 up a point in order

to both stay flat. The quantities are always going to offset, options are a zero sum game, so it becomes all about the urgency of the two sides.

And who has more urgency lately? Clearly the options shorts. So it stands to reason that the higher gamma gets, the more turbo in the stock.

The closer you get to expiration, the higher the gamma. And the more pressure on the side that is squeezed. In other words with a few days to go, maybe that gamma is 20. So a one point move causes the scrambling shorts to buy 2000, while the longs can sell 2000, probably at prices more their liking.

And what if it turns back down to the strike? The option shorts now have to sell back those 2000 shares to flatten out again. And so on and so forth.

And then the next day maybe they have 30 gamma near the money. Even more pressure in each direction exerted by the shorts in this environment.

Which brings us to Friday. Gamma is essentially infinity in the SPX August options. They have stopped trading. They are merely cashed out at the "opening" price (defined as whatever the calculation formula spits out taking the opening tick from each component). The rate cut and market pop comes an hour and change ahead of the open. All a call short can do to defend his position is chase futures/ETF's up. Some OTM calls he is short now have a 100 delta between now and the open. Sure there is an offsetting long that can sell the futures/ETF's, but who has the urgency here? Clearly the squeezed short. And thus the kindling wood lit by the Bernanke match.

Throw in a similar dynamic on all other index/ETF options that expire at the end of the day, and Big Ben literally found the perfect minute to cause the most pain to options sellers.

What happened that day? Worries about the financial crisis had begun to foment in the summer of 2007. We had a widespread perception of a Fed asleep at the switch. Jim Cramer's "He Has NO IDEA" rant on CNBC a couple weeks earlier received something like a billion YouTube viewings (okay, maybe not that many, but close). Then the Fed changed that perception in a big way with one shot across the bow, a surprise discount rate cut in the premarket of August 17. Expiration day. Could not have found a more brutal setup for options shorts than the August expiration cycle of 2007. Figure 6.1 shows a graph of the SPY from July expiration to August expiration.

And Figure 6.2 shows the VIX over that same time frame.

From the close of July expiration to the bottom on August 16, the SPY dropped about 12 percent, which in pre-2008 and prevolatility

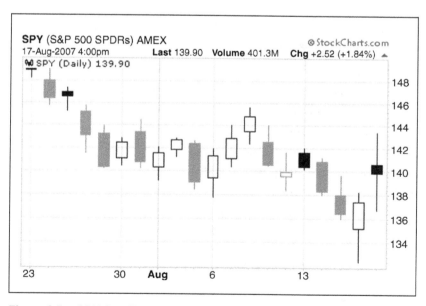

**Figure 6-1**    SPY Day Chart, August 2007 Expiration Cycle, Chart via StockCharts.com

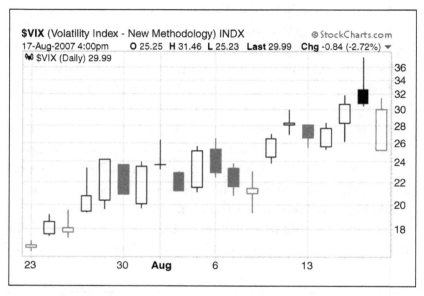

**Figure 6-2** VIX Day Chart, August 2007 Expiration Cycle, Chart via StockCharts.com

explosion days, was absolutely huge. Meanwhile, the VIX doubled. There was little doubt which side of the options trade scrambled into August 16. The surprise Fed move had to add a perfectly awful ending to an already difficult month.

So yes, plenty can go wrong with net selling options. Of course I use an extreme example here, but more to demonstrate the dynamics involved than to dissuade anyone from net shorting.

## So How Can Strong Volatility Work for Everybody?

How can strong volatility work for everybody? Well, what if we have a volatile and choppy environment? Lots of jigs, some decent moves, good daily ranges, but no particularly strong directional bias in the intermediate term. For Long Gamma Man, all sorts of opportunities to flip his stock, or stocks, intra day, provided, of course, that he recognizes the trading environment and acts somewhat accordingly.

Ms. Premium Seller would have to recognize the intermediate term picture and act accordingly as well. As a rule, traders should widen stops and price targets when volatility ticks up. Ms. Premium Seller should behave no differently. She should have discipline which involves picking her spots to make a few bad trades in order to defend her position, but she should also have a sense of the volatility and know not to trade as tightly when it picks up.

On any given day, we see "noise". By "noise" I mean gyrations in price that really have little meaning and scant relevance to future stock action. Long Gamma Man needs to capture as much of that noise as he possibly can. The greater the volatility, the greater the range of noise in the market, and the easier the task of Long Gamma Man to reel in some of it. Conversely, the very fact that it's noise means that it expressly behooves Ms. Premium Seller to ignore it and wait out the bigger picture lest she get shaken into more bad trades than she has to.

Skilled recognition by both parties of the unique trading backdrop could lead to positive returns for opposite sides of the same original options trade. And probably should lead to positive returns.

## What about Cheapening Volatility?

Cheapening volatility could work for both sides. Long Gamma Man sees little opportunity to flip stock intra day and figures he might as well sit on the sideline and let longer-term moves play out. Ms. Premium Seller does little to nothing or simply flattens out at the close each day and takes advantage of the fact that her position is ostensibly working.

It's a rough game though for both parties. If Ms. Premium Seller chooses the inaction route, she runs the risk of a few nonvolatile days in a row moving in the same direction. What she gains on the volatility crash, she loses on the rise of the intrinsic value of her options that she shorted.

Likewise, Long Gamma Man's only recourse is to sit and hope for the above event. There's no particular reason why low volatility will ultimately trend over a relatively short time frame. But that's his only path to profitability, hoping that's just what happens.

So the bottom line is that a high-volatility environment provides more price points, more returns to old price points, and just more action in general and more opportunity to make the correct play. It *can* happen in a low-volatility environment too; it's just not as likely.

## Summary

Options trading has many many moving parts. As a general rule, net selling options at a higher volatility than they ultimately realize will prove profitable. Likewise for net buying options at a lower volatility than realized.

But it's not that simple. Much depends on how the underlying stock gets from Point A to Point B, how the traders on each side of the trade manage their positions, and so on.

One thing to do is ignore anyone who throws numbers out trying to "prove" how much better you have it selling options compared to buying them. This tells an incomplete story. In general, options shorts do have the wind at their back in that they have daily attrition working in their favor. Most days they "win." But the losses tend toward the swifter and steeper, not to mention that they are open-ended. All things being equal, I do prefer selling options to buying them, but I always practice caution when playing that way.

In general, a high- or rising-volatility environment works best for all parties. One word. Opportunities. They are just way more prevalent for all parties when we see greater volatility.

Bottom line though is that volatility is just a statistic. There's nothing wrong with buying options at a high volatility if the ultimate realized volatility of the underlying justifies those high prices, provided you have a sufficient comfort level with managing just such a position.

# Chapter 7

# OPTIONS AND THE QUARTERLY EARNINGS REPORT

How about we have some actual fun with volatility? Let's take some of what we just learned as we entered the minds of long and short gamma traders and apply them to earnings season.

Bet you didn't know you can use an options screen to estimate market expectations for an earnings move.

Okay, you probably did know that. But I bet you didn't know how easy it is to gauge market expectations.

Perhaps I am ahead of myself here. Let's backtrack for a moment.

## Bid Me Up

Each and every quarter, pretty much the entire equity universe reports earnings. And those in the equity universe report roughly the same time within each quarter. Alcoa (AA) generally kicks things off on about the second week of a quarter, and then so on, until the lion's share report in the last two weeks of the first calendar month of the quarter. Expiration we know sits on the third Friday of the month, so the majority of earnings get reported in the second expiration cycle of each quarter. That is the February, May, August, and November cycles.

Most, but certainly not all, stocks have some uncertainty attached to that report. That uncertainty generally does not pertain to the actual earnings number. It used to, but along about the mid 1990s, some big tech companies discovered that if you underestimate your metrics to the analyst community and then "beat" the artificially reduced numbers when you actually report, the press and Wall Street will love it. It became a running joke, the old "beat by a penny game." Cisco was officially the lifetime achievement award winner in that department.

But I digress.

The real variables became *forward guidance* and *the tone of the conference call.* What did Company X think going forward? And that could really move a name?

For the most part, investors know when a given company will report. Even if not the precise date, they know which expiration cycle that report will fall in.

Why is that important?

As we said, there is a great deal of uncertainty about how a stock will react to guidance. And as such, options still alive at the time of the report get bid up a bit ahead of that uncertainty. The closer to expiration, the more the bid up in volatility terms, followed by the inevitable sell down after the news.

The degree of an options pre-earnings bid up will tell you just how far Mr. Market expects the stock in question to move after the report. Kind of an over/under, if you will. But it's essentially like regular volatility. Remember what just plain old volatility means? Divide it by the square root of 252 (the number of trading days per year), and it tells you the expected range that the underlying will fall within, 68 percent of the time.

When we estimate an earnings reaction, it's a similar sort of over/under. Most stocks will go "under." But the overs tend to dwarf the unders in magnitude such that, over the course of time, buying and selling options paper ahead of earnings should both have an expected gain of about zero.

## Do-It-Yourself Earnings Reaction Guesstimation

No matter whether you sit at a wildly sophisticated trading desk or use a dart board at home, you have one constant. If you want to gauge market estimates for an earnings reaction today, you will need to take a stab at estimating what happens to volatility tomorrow.

Sure a sophisticated firm can develop algorithms and models and all, but don't sell short your ability to eyeball a situation, use some intuition, and get a number in the same ballpark. It's rocket science, and yet it's truly not.

Here's what I do.

I peruse a volatility chart that I can get either for free or with a modest subscription charge. I can check recent volatility in options and in a particular stock itself, and get a sense of where options trade sans news. I would then factor in what is happening to volatility in the general marketplace and what's happening to other stocks that have already reported this cycle. If it's heavy, I would expect options volatility to cave to the low end of recent ranges. Likewise, if it's strong, I would not anticipate enormous overnight volatility slippage. You get periods like the fall of 2008 where general volatility remained so high that you would barely notice any company-specific news.

That will all give me a ballpark area guesstimate of where volatility would trade if we had no earnings uncertainty ahead of us.

I then take that guesstimate and analyze a handful of delta-neutral volatility plays like straddles and/or strangles. I can see on the board where that strangle trades now. How much will the stock have to move tonight, when combined with my estimate for volatility smackage will result in those strangles by and large opening up unchanged tomorrow.

Once I have that price, I have my personal estimate.

Pretty fuzzy, no?

Of course. But you'd be surprised at how accurate you can get with all that. No one knows exactly what volatility will do tomorrow. No one knows what actual market volatility will do tomorrow either.

And the point is that we don't get graded for nailing this to the penny. I use all this to get a general estimate. If I simply listened to the television, I'd hear shrieks and groans after each earnings gap, devoid of the slightest bit of context over whether the market pretty much anticipated this or not.

I use it also for my own trading. Does my "spider sense" tell me those magnitude estimates are too high? Often, yes.

And I use it also to see how stocks in general are moving relative to their expected ranges.

Earnings do not happen in a vacuum. Each earnings season tells a bit of a story. If an early-reporting batch of higher-profile names blasts or tanks on the reports, it logically puts a higher bid in the ensuing batch of names. Perhaps too much of a bid, and likely a decent time to look to sell options ahead of earnings.

## A Real Live Example

Figure 7.1 illustrates a one-year volatility chart for WYNN from May 2008. The lighter line represents normalized 30-day volatility of a hypothetical ATM option. At the time May options carried a mid 50s volatility. Where does volatility drop to after the news?

We have to consider several things. I normally expect volatility to decline to the low ebb of recent swings. But that low ebb is not too

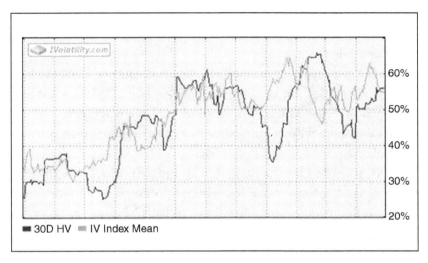

**Figure 7-1**  WYNN 30 Day Implied and Historical Volatility. May 2007-May 2008, Chart via Ivolatility.com

far down from where WYNN traded at the time, maybe a shade under 50.

We also need to see the volatility of WYNN itself. And that too has hovered near 50 over the past eight months.

And we need to see where longer-dated options trade. This is important because long-term options contain very minimal earnings bid up. They are essentially the "mean" to which the near-month options will likely "revert." This doesn't mean that the near-month options go exactly there. I mean it's possible that near-month options everywhere trade a significant premium or discount to outer-month options. So we'd want to adjust for that aspect too.

In WYNN, the December and January options were trading in the high 40s at the time.

Finally, we have to ask subjectively what else is happening around the volatility street? And the answer is that at the time was that things were not acting well at all. It was spring 2008, and the market had a temporarily better tone to it. And volatility across the floor traded on the heavy side.

WYNN was a tricky one. I rolled it all up and guessed that the May options would decline by about 10 volatility points to levels not seen since fall of 2007. The option trend at the time was down, and any names that saw anything but cosmic moves were getting hit more than normal.

Next, I would take that volatility and play (on paper) with some delta neutral options strategies, generally strangles. Suppose I sold them on the markets now. How far would WYNN have to move the next day such that if we factor in our anticipated volatility decline, the strangles would generally break even?

I threw numbers into the old options calculator available for free at ivolatility.com and determined that based on my volatility expectations, the over/under on WYNN was an approximately 10–12 percent move overnight. Pretty high for a normal big stock, but not cosmic for a relatively volatile one like WYNN.

## OK, How about Another Live Example

The chart in Figure 7.2 shows 30-day implied volatility in AAPL (lighter line) for a one-year period right up into the April 2008 earnings report. The darker line as always shows 30-day historical volatility.

Where will volatility go tomorrow? By tomorrow I mean tomorrow from the chart's perspective.

Well, there's pretty nice options runup into this report as you can see. Volatility near 60, which looks rather high compared to both AAPL options history and typical HV levels.

But then we have to ask the next question. What is going on in the overall volatility backdrop?

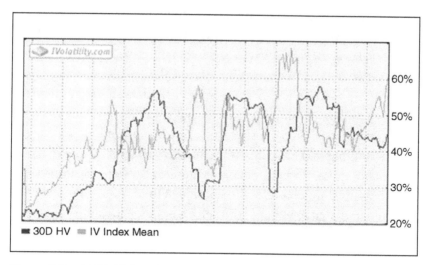

**Figure 7-2**   AAPL 30 Day Implied and Historical Volatility, April 2007-April 2008, Chart via Ivolatility.com

And similar to above in WYNN, it was a time in which stocks looked relatively okay and market volatility was in a decline phase. This suggests to me that the only thing holding AAPL options afloat is the imminent news. And we're primed for a decent decline. I'd eyeball this and guess low to mid 40s volatility, in line with recent lows in AAPL options, the HV, and longer-dated AAPL options.

I apply this to some straddles and strangles, and I come with an anticipated move in the 8–10 percent range. Perhaps a bit high for AAPL.

## Now What?

The above just provide me with guidelines. I find it useful to keep track, just as a general gauge of volatility trends. If the market perpetually overprices earnings moves, one can reasonably expect more docile future bid-ups. It's important to note though that by and large the market overprices more often than it underprices. But that certainly makes sense when you consider that the risk/reward picture here mirrors that picture from any decision tree that involves buying or selling options. Selling has an open-ended risk, thus shorts can demand modestly inflated premiums to offset that risk. The question though is more related to when that risk becomes grossly inflated. In some cycles we see nothing make an important move, in which case buyers go on a veritable strike. And prices fall for the next batch of earners.

Personally, I much prefer the sell side of this trade — in modest size and in names that report after the bell (as opposed to names that report pre opening).

Why the distinction?

Because if you want to sell options, you have to make preparations for the inevitable accidents — the guidance that goes off the charts, good or bad. And as such, you will have to defend your position at times and chase strength and short into weakness. The same way that Ms. Premium Seller has to do that in Chapter 6. The difference here is that we condense the expiration and decay cycle into one day.

And remember, like Ms. Premium Seller, we have a built-in margin for error. In the above example, we guesstimate that the market priced in a 10–12 percent move in WYNN overnight. Suppose now that WYNN blows the doors off on earnings and guides well, and the stock lifts 10 percent in the afterhours. I can now grudgingly chase and buy some there. If WYNN opens there the next day, I'll roughly break even at that level anyway as the volatility plunge in my short options should offset the increased intrinsic value.

If I wake up and see that the stock takes a second look and doesn't like what it sees and opens down from what I paid, I'll lose some on the bad stock trade. But I'll probably make more than that back as the strangle I sold gets plowed.

And what if I wake up and find that WYNN lifts even further?

Well, I have a loser on my hands, but at least I mitigated some of the loss with my stock purchase.

So by and large, I like having the safety net of the ability to hedge with stock in the afterhours. I understand I could do the same thing pre market, but I find that the noise and the risk of a complete whipsaw increases.

## Directions? We Don't Need Directions

Do you want to also figure out which way a stock moves on earnings?

I'd likely refrain from any options analysis on this one. The best rule is to assume that the trend in motion stays in motion. If a stock looks ugly heading into earnings, you probably need a whale of a report to change the tone. Of course we get dead cat "relief" bounces, but by and large, I would avoid fighting the trend.

However, I would assiduously shy away from analyzing options order flow ahead of a number. Say you see that OTM puts trading very actively a day or two ahead of earnings. Does this mean that the smart money knows disaster will strike? Maybe. But it also could mean that nervous Nellies want to hedge a long. If it's smart money, you'd want to short stock ahead of earnings, and conversely if it's unwarranted fear, you'd want to own the stock.

And here's problem number one. Options volume does not come with explanations of the thought process behind the order. We don't do exit interviews. Even if I stood in the crowd and saw the trade go up, I could not say for sure whether the buyer was wired in or a terrified long.

And here's problem number two. Even smart money can't know for sure what's already in a stock. Perhaps earnings = disaster. It's possible the stock had already whispered that in the price, in which case we may see a rally anyway. That sort of thing happened often to financials in 2008. News that was beyond bad accompanied a rally.

## And If Expiration Day Is Tomorrow?

If expiration day is tomorrow, you can throw all this estimation talk away and do something very simple. Look at near-month, near-money straddles and strangles. Yes, you have a full day's trade ahead of you, but options get to intrinsic really fast. I'd still look at the second month out to get a more exact guess (oxymoron alert), but by and large, the play will happen in the near month.

And, obviously, it's lightning in a bottle. There's no margin for error built in if you're wrong on this one because the play quickly becomes either a winner or loser.

And it's important to put this through the pinning lens (pins are when stocks close at a strike price on Expiration Day, we'll get into them in detail in Chapter 10) as well. A disappointing reaction in terms of magnitude will compound the tendency to pin. The options have that much more premium to absorb, and that much more downward pressure from the trapped longs.

Likewise, a large magnitude move will likely feed upon itself as trapped shorts get forced into the chase. Remember always that a move was already priced in, so this effect will happen only if the stock really gets going.

## Summary

You will never match the big fish given all the analytic tools at their disposal. But earnings magnitude estimation does not require exact precision. In fact even the most sophisticated modeling knows not what tomorrow brings.

And besides, what would you do with that info anyway?

It's nice to know that Mr. Market expects AAPL to move 9 percent tomorrow, but I would suggest that if you think AAPL will move 8.8 percent, you're not in there selling every option in sight. In fact I would suggest not selling any. None of these numbers will ever prove to be that exact, no matter how sophisticated the formula. The truth is that no one knows what the market or the stock or general volatility will do tomorrow.

I do run numbers to give me a sense of earnings magnitude expectations, and I make trading decisions through them, almost always of the sell variety. But to do that, I come prepared to defend my position and take my medicine when I have to, the same as if I simply shorted a "normal" options premium.

And I would exercise extreme caution attempting to derive direction from the options order flow. Put buyers, even the large ones, come in many stripes and with many motivations.

# Chapter 8

# LIKE THE WEATHER— THE TRADING VIX AND WHY IT DOESN'T DO WHAT YOU THINK IT DOES

We've learned a lot about timing and trading volatility in the last few chapters. Is there a simpler way to bet on volatility and/or hedge the risks associated with it?

Well, amid great fanfare, the CBOE introduced futures trading on the VIX in 2004. And in February 2006, options on the VIX. Before VIX options trading began, Bernie Schaeffer of Schaeffer's Research had this prescient analysis:

With the huge caveat that much will depend on the pricing of these new VIX options, I would (at least initially) advise against selling VIX calls or buying VIX puts. And buying VIX calls may prove to be prohibitively expensive. Selling VIX puts might prove to be an interesting proposition, as there is no explosive "event risk" that can blow up this trade and the case against a single-digit VIX is a strong one, regardless of future market direction.

And the good doctor did indeed prove correct as the VIX never got into single digits for any important length of time. And selling VIX calls ultimately proved disastrous, although the real pain in that trade did not occur for two-plus years.

But I digress. Lets' take a closer look at these trading pups, perhaps as confusing and confounding a product as there is listed on an exchange.

The big problem with VIX contracts?

Let me present you with some typical questions I've gotten in e-mails over the years.

Hey Adam:

I own these VIX April 50 calls. The VIX went up 10 points this week, and my calls didn't budge. Are the market makers screwing me over?

Hey Adam:

It's May, and I see the VIX here at 70. And I see November 40 calls trading at $13. Can't I just buy them and sell the VIX and pocket $17?

Hey Adam:

I am hearing about all this money everyone is making speculating on VIX calls. Should I play too?

Hey Adam:

How come pictures of models in bikinis come up any time you mention the VIX?

The answers were no, no, no, and the brand name of the bikini is actually "VIX." Really.

But I digress.

What's "wrong" with VIX products?

## They Don't Hedge What You Think They Hedge

The VIX estimates the implied volatility of an ATM option in SPX with 30 days of duration. A regular option on the SPX estimates the volatility of SPX itself between today and the day the option expires. Say it's May. You're looking at November options in SPX, and they trade at a 25 volatility. That is the volatility the market anticipates between now and November expiration.

A November VIX future? Quite different. That's an estimate of where the VIX will close on November expiration day. So if in May, you buy or sell a VIX November future or option, you are simply betting on where the VIX will settle on the morning of November expiration. A common misconception is that your bet is on volatility between May and November. Wrong. It's a bet on a single snapshot number that one day. And since the VIX itself is an estimate of volatility 30 days forward, a May transaction in a November VIX contract bets on where the market six month's hence will estimate volatility 30 days forward from there.

Oh, and did I mention that VIX futures and options close on a different day from regular futures and options? Yes, they expire 30 days ahead of the next month's regular expiration, which makes sense in a way since the VIX itself estimates the price of a 30-day option. The problem is that we have some four-week cycles and some five-week cycles, so that puts VIX expiration on either the Wednesday before or the Wednesday after regular expiration, depending on where regular expiration one cycle out sits.

Confused? You are not alone. Barron's Striking Price column ran the
following on June 10, 2006:

> IT SOUNDED GOOD IN THEORY. The VIX Volatility Index
> is a short-term forecast of stock-market volatility, and tends to
> jump when stocks sell off. So investors looking to hedge their
> portfolios would buy call options on the VIX, hoping these
> would appreciate when stocks slide.
>
> Reality proved quite different, however, as many flummoxed
> investors found out recently. As the S&P 500 pulled back 5% last
> month, the VIX—the CBOE Volatility Index—surged more
> than 50%, to its highest level in a year.
>
> Yet certain long-dated VIX calls barely budged, and their iner-
> tia has sparked quite a hubbub. "This is a freaking fraud!" one
> reader protested in an e-mail. If VIX were a stock, its sluggish
> calls—after such a big move in the underlying security—would
> be hard to fathom. But the VIX is a 30-day forecast of S&P 500
> volatility, as calibrated from index option prices, and, for all its
> popularity, is often misunderstood.
>
> VIX options are even trickier. Volume has soared since these
> were introduced in February, with 1.02 million VIX calls and
> puts trading in May—up from 285,994 in April. Yet they leave
> many investors perplexed.
>
> For a start, because VIX peeks only 30 days ahead, its current
> reading can differ substantially from its forward value. Case in
> point: Even as VIX climbed toward 19 early last week, futures
> prices pointed to a more subdued VIX, at about 16 come
> November—a sign the market expects the current volatility spike
> to moderate in time. This is logical, since projected volatility
> tends to jump sharply and then ebb gradually, and premiums
> soared recently in part because so many option sellers had scram-
> bled to cover their short-volatility bets.

Also, VIX options can only be exercised upon expiration. So a big jump in the VIX may not move longer-term call prices — if the market expects that jump to be fleeting. In other words, VIX options may not mirror real-time readings, although any divergence will decrease as options approach expiration. As a portfolio hedge, "buying VIX calls only helps in a crash right before expiration," says Tom Sosnoff, CEO of the brokerage firm thinkorswim Group.

Perhaps the best analogy to explain this is to think of the VIX futures /options as futures/options on the weather.

Pretend again it is May, and it's sunny and mild. And someone has a proposition for you.

No, it's not to go to a prom or a formal. It's to make a bet on the weather. In November. But not really November. He wants to make a bet on the average temperature of Al Roker's 30-day weather predictions. Predictions he will make in November. Six month's from now. Let's call him November Al Roker. And for argument's sake, we'll say Al Roker actually makes 30-day forecasts.

Now it's still May, and a cold front sets in. Very cold, record lows for May.

Will something like that cause you to guess that November Al Roker will lower his 30-day outlook? Probably not. You probably assume (rightly) that the May cold front is a blip, and not some sign of an impending ice age. It may affect trading on the June Al Roker, and, to a lesser extent, on the July Al Roker. But the further you get, the more you consider that the May cold front is just a blip and not some sign of a future trend.

Substitute VIX in the above for Al Roker and you get the gist behind the difficulty in pricing and understanding this product. And the incongruous nature of a bet here that few need to make.

## And Upon Expiration I Deliver You Nothing

VIX contracts settle for cash. Upon expiration, no security of any sort gets delivered. There's simply a cash transaction of the difference between where the VIX contract was bought/sold and where the VIX settles. And oh does that settlement get a bit tricky. And a bit "manufactured" at times. We get to that "manufactured" business later in the chapter.

But wait, there's more.

The above just considers VIX futures. But what about VIX options?

Yes, VIX options are actually options on the VIX future. They are a European exercise, meaning that you may not exercise them early. And like the futures, they cash settle. Take the second e-mail from earlier in the chapter ("It's May, and I see the VIX here at 70. And I see November 40 calls trading at $13. Can't I just buy them and sell the VIX and pocket $17?"), the apparent incongruity of a VIX option seeming to trade under parity.

The reality is that parity, like the owl in Twin Peaks, is not as it appears. VIX options trade off the corresponding VIX future, as we just said. VIX futures tend to assume mean reversion. Whenever the VIX deviates from a perceived normal level, VIX futures follow very slowly, just like our weather analogy. The further from expiration, the slower they follow the "cash" VIX and the longer they cling to some notion that they are the mean the cash reverts to.

So thus you're in a VIX lift. You get a situation where outer-month futures trade at deep discounts to the VIX itself. And since options price off the future, you will get situations in which certain outer-month calls trade at an apparent discount to the VIX.

It's actually a discount to the VIX, but that's just a meaningless construct since you can't exercise it. Nor would you want to as it prices off the already discounted future anyway.

Still want to trade these? Well we highlighted the difficulty in pricing an estimate or where future market makers will price volatility.

Now consider that a VIX option necessarily prices off the volatility of that estimate.

Yes, I will say it again. A VIX option prices off the volatility of a volatility estimate.

## And If VIX Futures and Options Do Not Do Enough for You?

On January 30, 2009, Barclay's added two new VIX products to the mix, ETNs under the symbols VXX and VXZ. According to Barclay's press release, "'VXX' is designed to track the S&P 500 VIX short-term futuresTM index TR which targets a constant weighted average future maturity of one month" while "VXZ" is designed to track the S&P 500 VIX midterm futuresTM index TR which targets a constant weighted average futures maturity of five months.

It's perhaps a better idea than futures, but keep in mind that, like futures, it will in exactly track the VIX you see on the board. Want some confusion though? We know that the VIX tracks a perpetual 30-day ATM option on SPX. A VIX future estimates where traders will price 30-day options on the day the future expires. The VIX ETF thus tracks a perpetual 30-day future on a perpetual 30-day option. And just to make it more interesting, Barclay's listed the ETNs with a starting price of 100, as opposed to say, a calculated price based on where the two near-month futures were that day of listing so we could more readily transpose them onto VIX values themselves.

All that being said, though, the shorter-term ETN, the VXX, provides a decent proxy for trading the VIX. It will lag actual VIX moves, but 30 days out will track it fairly well. And you can avoid the expiration day settlement games that we see in the VIX futures themselves. We detail this later in the chapter.

The VXZ? Stay away. There's no reason to bet on where the VIX will be five months from now unless you run a big derivatives desk. And again, if you must make that bet, I'm not sure what this provides beyond what you can do in the futures. And like futures, it will not price in volatility between now and expiration and is something that we might actually need to hedge.

## A Derivative of a Derivative of an Estimate of a Derivative Equals . . .

How volatile can, um, volatility get? Consider Figure 8.1, which is a graph of VIX volatility via ivolatility.com, covering from December 2007 through November 2008.

The darker line represents 30-day realized volatility of the VIX itself. In other words, if the VIX was a stock, the chart shows how much it

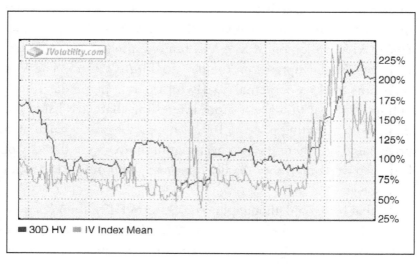

**Figure 8-1** 30 Day Volatility of VIX, December 2007-November 2008, via Ivolatility.com

actually moved. It was "relatively" peaceful until September as the stock generally hovered in the range of 50 to 100.

The lighter line shows implied volatility of the VIX options, basically a 30-day normalized ATM option. It's tricky defining exactly what constitutes an ATM option in VIX as noted earlier in the chapter. So you never want to look at this chart as anything but an estimate. But given that caveat, same as above, VIX volatility spent most of its time in a relatively tight range. Generally under 75.

And then fall of 2008 came. And VIX volatility lifted as high as 225.

So think about this if you had a position in VIX options. The VIX itself went from 20 to 80 over the course of three months or so, August to November. And options on the VIX tripled in volatility. A bad position, essentially anything involving short calls, got unfathomably bad given the double whammy of quadrupling VIX and tripling volatility of the VIX. Double whammy? That's more like a "duodecaphonic" whammy or something like that.

But of course, someone also had a terrific position. In fact that's one of the ostensible goals of this product. To allow some sort of "volatility" exposure into standard portfolios.

"What" you say? I mean doesn't owning actual puts give you volatility exposure? Or calls? Or merely handling a portfolio a certain way?

I guess not. You see, in 2007 the VIX awoke after about a four- to five-year slumber, and a school of thought arose that volatility had now become an asset class in and of itself. But the issue has two parts. One is whether volatility is indeed an asset class, and that really is just opinion, for which I do not have a strong one. The other is even *if* you believe volatility is an asset class, do you really believe that VIX options and/or futures provide the best way to expose yourself to that risk?

But first we must consider whether the second question is even worth asking. VIX options list on only one exchange, the CBOE, and that tends to keep markets on the relatively wide side. But what about the liquidity? Table 8.1 provides a view of the monthly volume in VIX options, as well as the share taken down by customers.

The table suggests nice growth early in the life of the product, growth that kind of crested in the fall of 2007 (perhaps resulting from

**Table 8.1**   VIX Option Volume Breakdown

|  | Total Volume | Call Volume | Put Volume | Customer% | MM% | Firm% |
|---|---|---|---|---|---|---|
| December 2006 | 560,997 | 462,967 | 98,060 | 46% | 33% | 21% |
| January 2007 | 624,829 | 496,161 | 128,668 | 47% | 29% | 24% |
| February 2007 | 866,495 | 691,711 | 174,784 | 58% | 22% | 21% |
| March 2007 | 1,575,245 | 1,363,964 | 211,281 | 49% | 25% | 25% |
| April 2007 | 1,111,136 | 668,736 | 442,400 | 52% | 29% | 19% |
| May 2007 | 1,569,794 | 1,156,293 | 413,501 | 57% | 21% | 23% |
| June 2007 | 2,000,936 | 1,613,850 | 387,086 | 53% | 27% | 20% |
| July 2007 | 2,628,601 | 2,044,587 | 584,014 | 50% | 28% | 22% |
| August 2007 | 3,576,129 | 2,659,411 | 916,718 | 49% | 31% | 19% |
| September 2007 | 2,315,379 | 1,742,033 | 573,346 | 46% | 31% | 24% |
| October 2007 | 2,751,499 | 2,022,920 | 728,574 | 47% | 35% | 18% |
| November 2007 | 3,086,525 | 2,275,591 | 810,934 | 46% | 36% | 18% |
| December 2007 | 1,281,803 | 928,642 | 353,161 | 48% | 37% | 15% |
| January 2008 | 2,184,959 | 1,686,574 | 498,385 | 50% | 35% | 15% |
| February 2008 | 1,995,487 | 1,491,360 | 504,127 | 51% | 38% | 11% |
| March 2008 | 2,070,771 | 1,598,444 | 472,327 | 49% | 37% | 14% |
| April 2008 | 1,998,618 | 1,547,069 | 451,549 | 53% | 35% | 12% |
| May 2008 | 1,940,083 | 1,505,304 | 434,779 | 51% | 39% | 10% |
| June 2008 | 2,255,171 | 1,708,837 | 546,334 | 50% | 37% | 13% |
| July 2008 | 2,571,456 | 1,975,951 | 595,505 | 52% | 37% | 10% |
| August 2008 | 1,968,665 | 1,203,272 | 765,393 | 52% | 37% | 11% |
| September 2008 | 3,286,269 | 2,419,722 | 866,547 | 51% | 43% | 6% |
| October 2008 | 3,154,589 | 2,011,141 | 1,143,448 | 47% | 42% | 11% |
| November 2008 |  |  |  |  |  |  |

Source: The Options Clearing Corp

increased popularity of Leveraged ETFs (see Chapter 14). To put this in context, we need to compare volume in VIX options to general volume trends. Let's compare it to the SPX, which is directly tied to the VIX, as the VIX actually measures volatility on the SPX.

And when you do that, you can see that the VIX peaked in relative popularity around November 2007. SPX traded about 31,482,590 contracts that month compared to 3,086,525 in the VIX. Contrast that with the market decline of October 2008. The VIX traded not much more than it did 11 months earlier, 3,154,589 vs. 3,086,525, whereas SPX traded a whopping 51,257,418 contracts.

So on the one hand the data in Table 8.1 tells us that volume in the VIX options did not pick up beyond the general ebbs and flows of options interest at a time when volatility itself exploded. On the other hand, customers comprise a greater share of the VIX market than they do in the SPX market. They take down roughly 50 percent of the VIX contracts compared to about a third in the SPX. And customers are precisely who should not trade these things.

Why?

Because they don't need them. Because there are better alternatives. And because tradable VIX products have hidden dangers beyond their typical scope.

## Is Any VIX Product the Most Effective Hedge for the Typical Investor?

Purchasing a VIX call hedges downside market exposure; that's not in dispute. And as Robert Whaley, creator of the VIX, notes, that the rate of acceleration in the VIX rises the more the market falls.

The fact that the VIX spikes during periods of market turmoil is why it has become known as the "investor fear gauge." Two forces are at play. If expected market volatility increases (decreases), investors demand higher (lower) rates of return on stocks, so stock prices fall (rise). This suggests the relation between rate of change in VIX should be proportional to the rate of return on the S&P 500 index. But, the relation is more complicated. Earlier we argued and documented that increased demand to buy index puts affects the level of VIX. Hence, we should expect to find that the change in VIX rises at a higher absolute rate when the stock market falls than when it rises.

To test this proposition, we regress the daily rate of change of the VIX, $t\,RVIX$, the rate of change of the S&P 500 portfolio, $t\,RSPX$, and the rate of change of the S&P 500 portfolio conditional on the market going down and 0 otherwise, $RSPXt$, that is

$$RVIX_t = \beta_0 + \beta_1 \Delta RSPX_t + \beta_2 RSPX_t + E_t$$

If our proposition is true, the intercept term should not be significantly different from 0, and the slope coefficients should be significantly less than 0. As it turns out, our predictions are true. The estimated relation between the rate of change of VIX and the rate of change in SPX is

$$RVIX_t = -0.004 - 2.990 \Delta RSPX_t - 1.503 RSPX_t$$

Where the number of observations used in the estimation is 5,753 and the regression R-squared is 55.7%. Except for the intercept, all regression coefficients are significantly different from zero at the 1% level.

The estimated intercept in the regression is –0.004, and the intercept is not significantly different from 0. This means that if the SPX does not change over the day, the rate of change in VIX should be negligible. This is not surprising. While the value of stocks is expected to grow through time in order to compensate investors for putting their capital at risk, volatility is not. Volatility tends to follow a mean-reverting process: when VIX is high, it tends to be pulled back down to its long-run mean, and, when VIX is too low, it tends to be pulled back up. The estimated intercept reflects the absence of deterministic growth. The estimated slope coefficients are both negative and significant, and clearly reflect not only the inverse relation between movements in VIX and movements in the S&P 500 but also the asymmetry of the movements brought about by portfolio insurance. The way to interpret the coefficients is as follows. If the SPX rises by 100 basis points, the VIX will fall by

$$RVIX_t = -2.990(.01) = 2.99\%$$

On the other hand, if the S&P 500 index falls by 100 basis points, VIX will rise by

$$RVIX_t = -2.990(.01) -1.503(.01) = -4.493\%$$

Because of the demand for portfolio insurance, the relation between rates of change in the VIX and the SPX is asymmetric. VIX is more a barometer of investors' fear of the downside than it is a barometer of investors' excitement (or greed) in a market rally. It is important to note, however, this evidence merely documents correlation and is not intended to express causality.

Okay, back to plain English.

If you are the 99.9 percent of the population whose eyes gloss over at those formulas, let's just take it at face value that the greater the market carnage, the exponentially greater the VIX will react.

But even given that, does a customer with a portfolio to protect benefit by hedging with a VIX call or future, as opposed to an SPX put or

SPY put, which we know will benefit from the direction via the price action and will indirectly benefit via the same acceleration mechanism in volatility. After all, how does the VIX lift? A rise in volatility in the SPX, as we know. And demand for portfolio insurance drives that very lift. So why make life complicated and go to the "second derivative" when you get every last tick of benefit owning the "first derivative," the put itself?

## Let the Games Begin

Oh, and did I mention that you have hidden dangers holding VIX contracts into expiration? How about the fact that you swim with the whales and sharks running giant derivatives portfolios, who know how to price every aspect of variance risk and who also have arbitraged positions on that they unwind and/or roll each expiration. Take the action on October 22, 2008, expiration day for the October VIX options.

I got the following e-mail a little after the open.

> Massive buyer of VIX strips today. look at nov. puts in spx— way down side—it is a stip of spx listed options that replicate the expiry vix oct future. Every strike from 300–1200 trades on a ratio. Puts to the downside and calls to the upside. You switch from calls to puts at the ATM strike. That looks like over 2 mm vega which is really big.
>
> . . . so basically someone rolled their long vega exposure out of vix oct futures into nov spx options.

In plain English, he's telling me about all sorts of trading interest in virtually every SPX series on the board. All on the market at the open. And boy was he correct. With the SPX over 950, a bevy of far OTM puts traded in major size. Table 8.2 shows what traded that open, courtesy of Bill Luby of VIX and More.

**Table 8.2** SPX Options Volume, October 22, 2008

| Strike | Contracts | Price | Time | $$$ | Strike | Contracts | Price | Time | $$$ |
|---|---|---|---|---|---|---|---|---|---|
| 300 | 47,339 | 0.15 | 9:30 | 710,085 | 730 | 1,989 | 11.20 | 9:31 | 2,227,680 |
| 350 | 33,000 | 0.15 | 9:30 | 495,000 | 740 | 2,576 | 15.80 | 9:38 | 4,070,080 |
| 375 | 24,419 | 0.20 | 9:30 | 488,380 | 760 | 2,445 | 18.10 | 9:31 | 4,425,450 |
| 400 | 21,658 | 0.25 | 9:30 | 541,450 | 770 | 1,788 | 15.90 | 9:30 | 2,842,920 |
| 425 | 19,536 | 0.30 | 9:30 | 586,080 | 775 | 1,178 | 16.80 | 9:30 | 1,979,040 |
| 450 | 17,425 | 1.30 | 9:32 | 2,265,250 | 780 | 1,740 | 18.40 | 9:31 | 3,201,600 |
| 500 | 14,117 | 1.50 | 9:34 | 2,117,550 | 790 | 2,269 | 19.00 | 9:34 | 4,311,100 |
| 525 | 12,802 | 1.60 | 9:33 | 2,048,320 | 805 | 1,092 | 22.00 | 9:30 | 2,402,400 |
| 550 | 8,166 | 1.90 | 9:34 | 1,551,540 | 810 | 1,076 | 23.30 | 9:30 | 2,507,080 |
| 560 | 4,500 | 2.90 | 9:35 | 1,305,000 | 815 | 1,064 | 24.10 | 9:30 | 2,564,240 |
| 570 | 3,258 | 3.10 | 9:35 | 1,009,980 | 820 | 1,049 | 25.40 | 9:30 | 2,664,460 |
| 580 | 2,100 | 2.55 | 9:35 | 535,500 | 825 | 1,038 | 26.30 | 9:30 | 2,729,940 |
| 585 | 2,063 | 3.50 | 9:36 | 722,050 | 830 | 1,026 | 27.30 | 9:30 | 2,800,980 |
| 590 | 2,026 | 4.50 | 9:36 | 911,700 | 835 | 1,012 | 28.40 | 9:30 | 2,874,080 |
| 595 | 1,992 | 4.90 | 9:38 | 976,080 | 840 | 1,014 | 29.00 | 9:30 | 2,940,600 |
| 605 | 1,931 | 3.20 | 9:30 | 617,920 | 845 | 987 | 31.00 | 9:30 | 3,059,700 |
| 610 | 1,896 | 5.30 | 9:36 | 1,004,880 | 855 | 966 | 33.40 | 9:30 | 3,226,440 |
| 615 | 1,866 | 5.70 | 9:39 | 1,063,620 | 860 | 963 | 34.70 | 9:30 | 3,341,610 |
| 620 | 1,835 | 5.70 | 9:37 | 1,045,950 | 865 | 943 | 36.10 | 9:30 | 3,404,230 |
| 625 | 1,809 | 4.20 | 9:30 | 759,780 | 870 | 942 | 37.80 | 9:30 | 3,560,760 |
| 630 | 1,780 | 4.50 | 9:31 | 801,000 | 875 | 922 | 38.20 | 9:30 | 3,522,040 |
| 635 | 1,751 | 4.70 | 9:30 | 822,970 | 880 | 923 | 40.60 | 9:30 | 3,747,380 |
| 640 | 1,724 | 4.80 | 9:31 | 827,520 | 885 | 900 | 42.20 | 9:30 | 3,798,000 |
| 645 | 1,697 | 5.10 | 9:31 | 865,470 | 890 | 902 | 43.20 | 9:30 | 3,896,640 |
| 655 | 1,647 | 5.50 | 9:30 | 905,850 | 895 | 881 | 45.60 | 9:30 | 4,017,360 |
| 660 | 1,619 | 6.70 | 9:35 | 1,084,730 | 905 | 861 | 49.70 | 9:31 | 4,279,170 |
| 665 | 1,598 | 6.00 | 9:30 | 958,800 | 910 | 852 | 51.80 | 9:31 | 4,413,360 |
| 670 | 1,572 | 7.20 | 9:35 | 1,131,840 | 915 | 842 | 53.30 | 9:31 | 4,487,860 |
| 675 | 1,550 | 6.70 | 9:32 | 1,038,500 | 920 | 833 | 55.70 | 9:31 | 4,639,810 |
| 680 | 2,290 | 9.10 | 9:37 | 2,083,900 | 925 | 585 | 56.60 | 9:31 | 3,311,100 |
| 690 | 2,964 | 9.60 | 9:36 | 2,845,440 | 930 | 589 | 59.40 | 9:31 | 3,498,660 |
| 710 | 2,799 | 11.50 | 9:37 | 3,218,850 | 935 | 220 | 62.00 | 9:31 | 1,364,000 |
| 720 | 2,044 | 10.10 | 9:31 | 2,064,440 | | | | | |
| | | | | | TOTAL | 285,240 | | | 145,515,195 |

The number at the bottom of the table, $145,515,195, is roughly the money spent on OTM puts in SPX that morning.

Why would someone spend all that money buying puts that will mostly go worthless even in the ugliest of markets?

Well, the VIX October options and futures cashed out that morning. The SPX dropped by about 3 percent on the open of October 22, and volatility exploded out of the gate. The VIX eventually settled that open at 63.22, up nearly 10 points.

But $145 million? To put that into perspective, the VIX October 25 calls alone increased in value by some $100 million from Tuesday's close to Wednesday's settlement price. VIX Oct. 60 calls closed at small change Tuesday and looked like rip-ups; then they got cashed out at $3.22.

And also remember that the $145 million is not a pure expense; the SPX puts all have 30 days of life, and many retain some value.

So, a question begs asking. Did someone rig the system to profiteer on his or her VIX calls? Possibly, but also possibly not. The market did gap down large that morning, and times were as shaky as ever. So it's possible that the VIX opens there anyway. It's also possibly part of an unwind where both sides roll a trade.

But that's not the point for average customers. They're just sitting ducks in all this, at the mercy of where a few big players print all these SPX options. It may not matter to the big fish where the VIX actually settles as it is likely offset equally by another side of a complex trade somewhere. To Joe the small VIX player though, the whole month may come and go based on the whims of one unwind. Not a position people should leave themselves in.

## You Really Want to Trade These Pups Head On

The VIX is all about mean reversion. That mean can, of course, move, as we show later in the chapter, but as a general trading strategy, fading "noise" and flattening at a mean (maybe defined as a moving average) sure seems like a solid approach.

Rob Hanna at the Quantifiable Edges Web site ran some hypotheticals through his database, and came back with this:

I've seen some articles in the press over the last few months suggesting that one way to profit in volatile markets is by trading VIX options. They typically make it sound easy. "You don't even need to know the direction of the market. You just need to determine whether volatility is likely to rise or fall. If you think volatility is going higher, you can buy VIX call options. If you think it's going lower, you can buy VIX put options." The problem with this logic is that VIX option prices do not follow the VIX index. They follow VIX futures prices. A couple of months ago I decided to quantify how much this really matters.

It is well known by traders that the VIX has a strong tendency to oscillate. Therefore, when people consider trading the VIX, they many times think mean-reverting strategies will work best. I took some simple mean-reverting strategies and applied them to the index to see what kind of returns I would get. Two examples were: 1) Short the VIX if it closes 15% or more above its 10-day moving average. Cover when it closes below its 10-day moving average. 2) Short the VIX if it closes at a 10-day high. Cover when it closes below its 10-day moving average. In both cases the opposite stretch would apply for purchases. Not surprisingly, they worked. What was intriguing was HOW WELL they worked. I then combined these strategies with a few others to create an indicator which would signal to me when the VIX was stretched and due for a reversal.

Assuming you treated the VIX as a security and allocated a certain dollar amount whenever you bought/shorted it, over the last 3 years my simple system would have returned about 170% per year based on raw returns (no commissions or slippage).

It sounds pretty awesome, but here's the rub. That trade assumes you can actually sell a cash VIX. Unfortunately you can't, nor will you likely ever be able to. You need to buy/sell VIX futures and/or options and/or ETNs that track the near-month futures. And remember, they all assume every move is a blip, until proven otherwise.

So what happens when you take the signals from the above example, but trade an available VIX product at that moment?

> Now, to see the effect that trading futures would have on the system, I downloaded all the historical data from CBOE and ran the trades through using front month futures. I performed rollovers those times when the future expired before the trade closed. Note that the entry and exit triggers were based on the action in the VIX—not in the futures. The purpose of the study was to see whether someone could trade futures/options based on the action in the VIX index. The results? Instead of returning 170%/yr over the last 3 years, the system now returned 5% total!! Factor in some commissions and slippage and my incredible system is now a money-loser.

And therein lies the problem. This of course does not comprise the only trading strategy, not by a long shot. But it does highlight the difficulties of gaming a product with so many moving parts.

## So What about Just Buying Volatility on, Well, Volatility?

What do I mean by buying volatility on volatility? I mean go long gamma in VIX options. As a very very very general rule, options ownership works when you buy options at an implied volatility that proves cheaper than the realized volatility between now and when those options expire. We went over this concept in depth in Chapter 6.

So taking a look at the chart from earlier in the chapter that appears to happen in VIX options on a regular basis. The lighter line (implied volatility) virtually always runs below the darker line (realized, or historical, volatility).

But alas, there's a catch. Isn't there always a catch?

Remember again, for the umpteenth time in this chapter, you can't buy and sell the actual VIX, only the futures/ETNs in this case. And since the futures/ETNs always assume some sort of mean reversion, they'll *always* lag moves in the VIX itself. So the "cheapness" of VIX options mislead, as the VIX futures/ETNs will not typically move far enough or fast enough to flip for sufficient profits so as to offset the daily cost, the time decay, of owning VIX options paper.

In fact, it's not much different here from a regular stock. Most regular stocks tend to overprice options relative to realized stock volatility for the lion's share of the time. This accounts for the occasional outlier event.

## So Maybe Options Here Are a Net Sale?

I don't trade VIX options. In fact I have never traded a VIX option. My strong preference when I want to make a "bet" on volatility is to make it a more direct play and actually buy or sell options on the underlying product itself. In other words, if I believe that the market itself underpriced volatility, I would buy options on SPY or QQQQ or IWM or some direct offshoot of one of those, like an Inverse or 2x product.

If you forced me to trade a VIX product, I would go net short options. Period. In fact I can't think of a circumstance in which I would want to own paper. Again, if I believe volatility will move soon, I will play it much more directly.

But let's say I find volatility too cheap, and I buy some straddles or strangles in SPY. Almost by definition, I have the opinion that realized volatility will exceed the implied volatility I just paid for. But let's say I am worried that the implied volatility of the options may decline anyway. What trade would fit that whole combo of thought? Shorting VIX calls. If I am wrong on that end, I more than make it up via the volatility increase in the SPY options I own. Not to mention the fact I have probably also made money flipping SPY itself against those options.

Now scratch that, reverse it, and say I got bearish on index volatility and shorted SPY straddles and strangles. I expect realized volatility to decline. But am worried implied volatility that I sold ticks up anyway. I could argue for owning VIX calls in that circumstance, but I would personally rather sell VIX puts. The play on the SPY options is designed to collect some daily decay, so do I really want to offset that by paying decay in VIX options? Not really. I'd sooner pocket more decay against the likely cost I have defending my SPY options short via chasing SPY itself.

## Any Trading Signals You Can Derive from the VIX Trading Products?

So you're wondering whether there are trading signals you can derive from the VIX products. Glad you asked. The answer is "not really." But they do have some utility.

A VIX future effectively serves as a mean reversion indicator in that it tells us what the market expects as a mean. And early in the life of the VIX future, really until 2008, that mean "magnet" seemed to work more often than not. VIX spikes were met with relative futures indifference and a subsequent erasure of the spike back to the perceived mean.

But it was a bit of fool's gold.

For one thing, you didn't need a future to tell you the market considers every move in the VIX noise until proven real. Longer-dated options can tell us that. And we have had them basically forever.

Check out the three graphs in Figure 8.2. They show implied volatility (lighter line) of a normalized ATM option in SPY over dif-

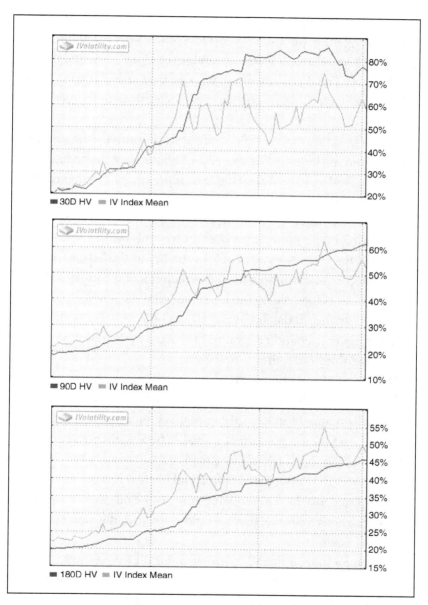

**Figure 8.2**    30, 90 and 180 Volatility of SPY September–December 2008, via Ivolatility.com

ferent time frames. Each runs from early September 2008, just before the huge volatility run up, to early December. The first graph (on the top) shows a 30-day option, the second (center) a 90-day, and the third the 180-day. The dates line up, so you can look at each on top of each other. The darker line shows historical volatility over the given time frame.

All three sat in the low 20s at the start, essentially the perceived equilibrium at the time. By the end of September however, the 30-day had soared to 40, which at the time represented a multi-year high. Longer-dated options considered it a blip at that point. The 90-day went a smidge north of 30, while the 180-day was about 30.

And then came the real fireworks. Over the next two months we witnessed three blasts to around 70 volatility in the 30-day measure. And here's the interesting part. The perception of the mean increased each time, as evidenced by the longer-dated ones. The first blip to 70 volatility saw the 90-day hit about 50, and the 180-day nudge to the mid 40s. By the second go around they were up to about 58 and 48, and by the third time, they were 62 and 55.

What does this demonstrate?

For one thing, the notion of mean reversion in volatility persists no matter what happens in the options marts. It's just the mean itself that changes. And there's no correct spread between any given durations. And no trading signal when the spreads get out of whack. Nine times out ten, the VIX shorter-dated option will likely revert back to the pricing suggested by the longer-dated one. But that outlier can be so severe, as in this example, that it would wash away any perceived edge in trading against it.

Oh, and a look at the VIX, which is, for all intents and purposes, the same thing as the 30-day IV above, against VIX futures would tell the exact same story as the above. The VIX shot up, and the futures lagged and lagged and lagged before traders came to grips with the notion that the volatility run up in the fall of 2008 was real.

But that's not to say that the VIX futures lack utility.

That mean reversion assumption has value in and of itself. Consider a preholiday stretch when we expect light option demand and a "cash" volatility reading that understates real volatility. A VIX future will essentially ignore it all as a blip and give a purer reading concerning volatility expectations. Remember that future prices the VIX on a snapshot and the perceived blips between here and there will not disrupt that snapshot.

## Summary

Rare is it that a product comes down the pike so well-timed as these tradable VIXs. When they began, awareness of all things volatility had gone from close to zero to on the radar. Within a couple of years, volatility interpretation became all the rage, and here was a way to directly play it.

2007 saw the VIX double, from low teens to mid-20s. 2008 saw the VIX almost quadruple at its peak.

So this sounds great to play, right?

Well, for a variety of reasons, what seemed simple was in fact far more complex than first met the eye. VIX contracts base on VIX futures, and VIX futures do not move in perfect unison with actual volatility. In fact there are times when they don't react at all. And they do not confer delivery of any actual product as they cash settle upon expiration, which puts the owner or seller at risk of a somewhat random runoff on expiration day that derives that cash value.

VIX ETNs at least avoid expiration risks, but they still can't quite solve the imperfect correlation problem.

Investors and all but the most sophisticated traders are better served keeping it simple and using plain old index and ETF puts and calls to hedge portfolios and/or speculate on market action. After all, that's what the VIX tracks to begin with.

Volatility has a partner in crime in the options data world good old put/call ratios. Can we augment analysis of one with data from the other and find more hidden option truths? Let's take an extended look.

# Chapter 9

# RATIO, RATIO

We have spent a boatload of time so far on the minutia of all things volatility. But we have another chain of options analysis metrics.

The put/call ratio.

The theory behind a put/call ratio is very simple. Puts represent bearish bets or hedges, and calls represent bullish ones. The higher the ratio, the more bearish the lean in options. And the more bearish the lean, the more bullish for the market since this is a contra indicator.

I'm going to do this discussion of put/call ratios a little backwards and begin with the ending, my preexisting conclusion. I don't believe in their forecasting value in any important way, basically because I don't believe the data will ever actually jibe with the theory. This will certainly not happen without tweaking. And even there, I see flaws. Then I will try to prove myself utterly wrong, or at least a bit misguided.

## So What's My Problem with This Fine Measure?

A basic put/call assumes that the initiator of the trade bought the option. But if you believe that what you don't know can hurt you, then we have to say that what we don't know about a simple put or call print on a screen can simply kill you. So let us note what we don't know.

1. We know not whether the order initiator actually bought the option — maybe a block of calls traded as part of a covered write. The "write" part is obvious so, I guess, I should change "maybe" in the last sentence to "likely," because buy-writing remains now and probably always has been the most popular use of options for a retail investor. The very investor you want to fade, at least if you believe in the concept of a put/call ratio. And if the investor is selling call options, he's doing something bearish, so contrary you wants to trade bullishly. But the options print as calls, so they would lower the put/call ratio, which is actually bearish.

2. We don't know whether the initiator was opening or closing. Presumably an opening order has more significance.

3. Even if we know the side of the initiating offer, we don't know the actual bet being made. Say it's a buy-write, but it's the whole package at once — options and stock. The initiator presumably has done the buy-write side. So she has effectively shorted puts. Yet the trade prints as a call.

4. This leads to another point. Calls are often puts in disguise, like a buy-write. And likewise, puts are often calls in disguise if they get packaged with stock.

5. We don't know whether the options are part of some sort of spread. Maybe the initiator is rolling short calls from a buy-write into another month. Maybe he's trading a vertical spread. These trades mislead in two ways in that they both double the volume of whichever side the initiator used, and they are only modestly directional in nature.

6. We don't know who traded the option. We have retail money, which this theory says you want to fade (take the other side of). We have smart, wired-in money that you want to basically piggyback. If one or the other buys puts, they will print the same

way and go into a generic ratio in the same way, yet knowledge of who actually initiated the order makes all the difference in the world as to whether we should read it bullishly or bearishly.

7. We don't know whether the order stands alone or hedges something else. Is the buyer speculating on puts (bullish to us, from a contrary perspective) or simply hedging a long stock or index (modestly bearish if she's doing it in order to stay long).

8. We don't know how much volume had absolutely no economic value whatsoever. Like a dividend spread where two traders cross call verticals in monstrous size, and then each exercises what he or she bought and hopes not to get assigned the calls that each sold. This is like those SPX put prints on the open on VIX expiration day that we learned about in Chapter 8 that merely serve to set a settlement value on the VIX. Or it may be something as simple as two traders in an options crowd crossing a spread or combo to clean up a long or short position. That very thing actually happened once when I was a market maker in Caterpillar options. Two traders crossed a large-sized call spread. One was taking an extended vacation and wanted a smaller position. About an hour later, we saw a CAT story on the tape analyzing the increased call volume and how it represented some sort of understandable bullish bet in the stock. Say what? It was nothing of the sort.

9. We have many free and paid services out there that report unusual trading volume in a given class or series. We think of these as tells we *want* to join, not contrary tells. Say that word gets around about large call buying in stock XYZ. The implication is that this is bullish and you want to go long XYZ. Yet obviously that same call volume goes into the CBOE put/call reading and lowers it on the margins, turning it more bearish. How do we resolve that anomaly?

## These Numbers We All Refer To

My criticism relates to the basic put/call stat that everybody quotes—
the numbers popped out by the CBOE.

These numbers are broken up into equity and nonequity slices.
Index hedges have different characteristics from equity hedges and are
often quite skewed to the put side. The all-equities number gives a
cleaner look, so that's what we will use for analysis.

The graph in Figure 9.1 charts this ratio for 2008.

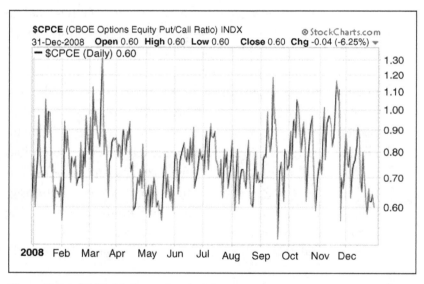

**Figure 9-1** CBOE All Equity Put Call Ratio for 2008, via StockCharts.com

A cursory glance at the chart shows that it does at the very least rein-
force what we know about the market at a given time—to a point. It
spiked in March at a temporary bottom—Bear Stearns implosion
week. But otherwise it really hovered within a relatively small range
amidst what turned into a gigantic year for volatility.

Given all my critiques, I expected scant relationship between movement in the put/call ratio and movement in the market. But lo and behold, it's not that bad. Using the all-equities number and data from October 2003 to the end of 2007 provided by the CBOE, I found a .3491 correlation between the 10-day SMA of the put/call and the performance of the SPX over the next 30 days. But does that really tell us anything beyond what we already know? The following from Michael Stokes at MarketSci Blog suggests not:

> I've never quite figured out a magic bullet for using the put-to-call ratio in my own trading, but one thing I can say with quite a bit of confidence is that predicting the direction of the put-to-call ratio (or whether bullish/bearish sentiment is increasing or decreasing) is of almost no trading value.
>
> How can I be so sure? Because predicting the direction of the put-to-call (PCR) ratio is incredibly easy, but the market doesn't react much differently when we predict the PCR to increase or decrease. This is of course counter-intuitive: an increasing PCR should be an indicator of bearish sentiment (and vice-versa).
>
> The graph [Figure 9.2] shows the PCR and the "trading" results of a simple strategy for predicting when the PCR will increase and decrease. I know that you can't actually trade the PCR—this is just a mental exercise—but the point should be obvious. The put-to-call ratio is the most predictable financial instrument I've ever encountered.
>
> My "strategy" for predicting the PCR. I expect the PCR to increase/decrease from today's close when the 4-day EMA of the PCR is below/above the 4-day SMA. Between mid-1995 to the present, this strategy correctly predicted the following day's direction 63.8% of the time with correct predictions 1.44 times larger than incorrect ones.

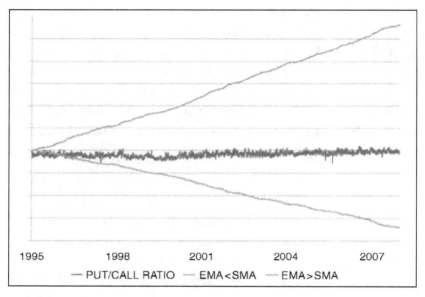

1995          1998          2001          2004          2007

— PUT/CALL RATIO    ⋯ EMA<SMA    ⋯ EMA>SMA

**Figure 9-2**

If the PCR were actually a measure of bullish versus bearish sentiment, and we were able to accurately predict the direction of the PCR (as I did above), then we should also be able to predict the shifting sentiment of the market, right? Not so fast.

The graph [Figure 9.3] shows the S&P 500, and the results of trading the S&P 500 using our increasing and decreasing PCR predictions from mid-1995 to the present. Did the market perform worse when we predicted the PCR to increase (read "more bearish sentiment")? Sure, a bit. Stats below [Figure 9.4].

But was this difference enough to call the put-to-call's direction a useful market timing indicator? I don't think so.

But then like manna from heaven, or at least like a new index from an MBA, the ISEE (ISE Sentiment Index) was born. It was the brain-

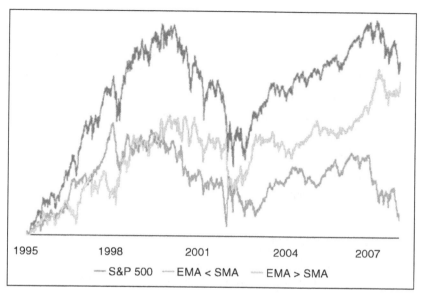

**Figure 9-3**

| Statistic | S&P 500: Buy and Hold | S&P 500: Predict PCR Inc. | S&P 500: Predict PCR Dec. |
|---|---|---|---|
| Annualized Return | 6.6% | 0.6% | 5.9% |
| Annualized Std. Dev. | 17.6% | 12.0% | 12.8% |
| Sharpe Ratio | 0.15 | -0.28 | 0.15 |

**Figure 9-4**

child of the International Stock Exchange, the first all-automated options mart. It was as if it read my concerns from above and addressed as many as humanly possible. The ISE described it as follows:

The ISE Sentiment Index (ISEE) is designed to show how investors view stock prices. The ISEE only measures opening long customer transactions on ISE. Transactions made by market makers and firms are not included in ISEE because they are not considered representative of market sentiment due to the often specialized nature of those transactions. Customer transactions, meanwhile, are often thought to best represent market sentiment because customers, which include individual investors, often buy call and put options to express their sentiment toward a particular stock.

Bravo. Bravo.

Sounds wonderful. I mean no more smart money. Only buyers. Etc. Etc. It sure seems like a far better mousetrap. In fact my only quibble is that it is reported as a call/put ratio. And then it must be multiplied by 100, which needlessly adds confusion when you try to compare it to the CBOE's basic put/call.

Sure sounds like a better mousetrap. But then I run a simple correlation between the 10-day Moving Average and the 30-day returns in SPX as above, and it's –.04 (remember it's a call/put, so a high negative number would be stronger).

Ouch.

## What's Going On?

I suspect that some sample size errors hurt the ISEE number. Not in the data as it goes back long enough in time and through enough different market regimes to make some judgments. Rather, it just does not have enough data on the day-to-day. The theory appears sound to me. It's a contrary sentiment indicator. So pick and choose the volume you actually want to isolate and fade.

But even so . . .

Perhaps I should reconsider my interpretation and stick with the CBOE number. Forget the how and why behind an options order. Could it be that someone choosing to trade a put or call, for whatever reason, is a contrary tell? I mean in a down market, puts simply trade with more liquidity. Even if I want to buy a call, I may find trading it synthetically, buying puts vs. stock, gets me better fills on a down day. So I may use puts instead.

But if that's the case, it suggests that a put/call ratio does not tell us anything we don't already know. I mean you could simply assume that we can look at it another way. If the market goes lower, put volume will logically increase relative to call volume. So if the market simply going lower predicts the market going higher, then we can infer that the excess put volume is more a by-product of that lower market and not a particularly insightful prediction of future market direction.

For example, if instead of looking at a 10-day MA of the put/call ratio, we just ask whether the performance in the last 10 days in the market "predicts" the next 30 days forward. Just in reverse. And it does, although only about half as well as the put/call ratio. It has a correlation of –.18123. So it looks like there's actually something there.

Could it be options volume in general? You just simply get busier in the options markets when emotions get extreme. And that often coincides with actual turns.

Dr. Brett Steenbarger has some support for this thought, from his blog posting on May 12, 2007:

When we have more puts and more calls trading, we can reasonably assume that speculators are active in the marketplace and emotions are running strong. Conversely, very low option volume suggests more placidity among speculators.

I went back to the beginning of 2005 (N = 573 trading days) and expressed each day's equity option volume as a proportion of the prior 200 days' moving average. I then assessed how a 10-

day moving average of this relative volume was related to future price change in the S&P 500 Index (SPY)

When option volume over a 10-day period was 25% or more ahead of its 200 day moving average (N = 92), the next 10 days in SPY averaged a very solid gain of .89% (66 up, 26 down). It thus appears that, when emotions are frothy among stocks, returns have been skewed to the bullish side.

Sounds about right. But then he continues with this:

When option volume over a 10-day period was below its 200 day moving average (N = 123), the next 10 days in SPY averaged an impressive gain of .85% (90 up, 33 down). Interestingly, very low emotionality among speculators has also been associated with a bullish bias.

Well, back to square one. I suspect that when the market already acts well, volume simply dries up in the options. Why hedge anything? I mean volatility has likely dropped, and stocks have done well. Good stock action has probably led to reduced options activity, not the other way around.

## How About If We Relate the Put/Call to Volatility?

It stands to reason that we would find a pretty strong relationship between the put/call and volatility. After all, what is a volatility spike but a run on puts?

And sure enough we find one.

Examining the same data set from October 2003 through the end of 2007, we find 98 trading days where the put/call closed at least 20 percent above it's 20-day MA. On those same days, the VIX closed an average of 10 percent above its own 20-day SMA (with a median reading of 8 percent above). Likewise, in 90 instances over that same stretch where the put/call closed 20 percent or more below the 20-day SMA, the VIX closed an average of 5 percent below its own 20-day SMA.

So here's a thought. Let's split the 98 extended high put/call days into two halves, one where we see the VIX 8 percent above its 20-day SMA, and the other where we see the VIX below that threshold. And we'll see how the market does 15 and 30 days out on average. Since these results obviously will cluster, we will stipulate that we can take only one signal per week.

And bingo. We do have a decent signal. On those days where the put/call closed more than 20 percent above its MA and the VIX closed more than 8 percent above its 20-day MA, the SPX had an average return of 1.03 percent over the next 15 days, and 1.73 percent over the next 30 days. In those instances where the VIX rose by less than 8 percent, the SPX rose an average of .0011 percent over 15 days and declined by –.0006 percent over 30 days.

We totaled 26 observations on the high VIX/high put/call setup. The market was higher 18 times 15 days out, and 18 times 30 days out (not always the same observation). The maximum win was 5.36 percent 15 days out, but the maximum loss was greater, –5.559%. Likewise the maximum 30-day win was 7.44 percent versus a 7.17 percent maximum loss.

Next we have to ask whether these are simply times when the SPX is already extended down, and the put/call and VIX explosions tell us something we don't already know.

And surprisingly, it doesn't. On average, the SPX sits 1.81 percent below its 20-day SMA on those 26 dates. Not exceptional.

So it all sounds great. But what if similar to what we saw in the total options volume study above, a particularly low put/call also can have bullish tidings.

I continued this experiment in reverse. I looked at dates where the put/call closed 20 percent or more below its 20-day SMA. There were a total of 90 observations. The median VIX in the observations traded 5 percent below its 20-day SMA. Again, we divided it into high and low VIX halves and stipulated only one observation per week so as not to duplicate the same measurement.

In theory, the market should act poorly, especially in times of low put/call and low volatility. But no. In 24 observations, we see pretty flat market returns. Then 15 days later, the average SPX return is .33 percent, and after 30 days, it's .20%. Really nothing.

But here's the semi surprise. In the 28 observations where the put/call closed 20 percent below its 20-day MA and the VIX was greater than 95 percent of its own 20-day SMA, the market returned an average of 1.19 percent 15 sessions later, and a very impressive 2.28 percent 30 sessions later. The market rallied 21 of the 28 times after 15 days, and 20 of 28 after 30 days. Before we get too comfortable though, it did stumble into an 8.56 percent bath in 15 sessions on a signal generated in October 2007.

In other words very low relative put volume combined with relatively high VIX (it's not really high, since many times it was below its 20-day SMA) predicted pretty much the same for the market as a high put/call, high VIX.

So we've established a sort of rule here. If the put/call deviates by 20 percent from its 20-day SMA and the VIX is relatively high, it's a decent time to do something a little bullish.

## Random Noise?

But I have problems with this sort of analysis. Put/call on a single day has too much noise. Plus we just used moving averages of daily put/call closes rather than properly weighting the total put and total call volume. We're onto something here, so let's refine the methodology. We will measure put/call over a 4-day period and divide it by put/call over a 20-day period.

Table 9.1 shows the 15-day and 30-day returns over different conditions. Same data set as above, same conditions. Only one observation allowed per week. VIX versus 20-day MA, broken in two parts so as to split samples roughly into high and low VIX.

It's pretty clear that we got some decent returns when buying when we saw an extended put/call in concert with an extended VIX. Unlike the single-day sample, we did okay owning stocks when we had a

**Table 9-1**  4-Day Put/Call vs. 20-Day Put/Call vs. VIX

| | 4-Day P/C 10% above 20-Day VIX >9% above 20-Day SMA | 4-Day P/C 15% above 20-Day VIX<9% above 20-Day SMA | 4-Day P/C 15% above 20-Day VIX>11% above 20-Day SMA | 4-Day P/C 15% above 20-Day VIX<11% above 20-Day SMA | 4-Day P/C 10% below 20-Day VIX>93% of 20-Day SMA | 4-Day P/C 10% below 20-Day VIX<93% of 20-Day SMA |
|---|---|---|---|---|---|---|
| Observations | 17 | 28 | 12 | 10 | 24 | 23 |
| 15-day average return | 1.17% | .05% | 1.9% | .28% | .5% | 1.29% |
| Low 15-day return | −7.34% | −3.67% | −4.81% | −2.13% | −5.28% | −1.10% |
| High 15-day return | 5.36% | 4.59% | 5.36% | 4.59% | 5.02% | 5.28% |
| 30-day average return | 3.16% | .2% | 4.15% | .51% | .49% | 1.47% |
| Low 30-day return | −3.15% | −4.17% | −1.96% | −3.09% | −6.10% | −7.69% |
| High 30-day return | 8.86% | 5.05% | 8.18% | 5.05% | 6.50% | 5.47% |

depressed put/call and depressed volatility combo. It makes sense in a way in that complacency tends to linger and that this coincides with slow upward-moving markets.

I did not look for maximum drawdowns. What I did do though was extend the experiment into the year of drawdowns, 2008.

We generated five signals, including one on September 12 that resulted in a nearly 12 percent loss 15 trading days out, and a lovely 30 percent hit 30 days out.

## System of an Up

The above all sounds good. I mean high put/call and high volatility equal good returns, especially if you put your finger over the 2008 debacle. But this doesn't actually produce actionable information. We have overlapping buys and our "out" depends on a somewhat arbitrary time frame. What if we come up with some sort of system?

How about this. We go long when the four-day put/call goes 15 percent above the 20-day *and* the VIX closes at least 8 percent above its 20-day MA. We exit when both the 4-day put/call ratio dips below the 20-day ratio *and* when the VIX closes below its 20-day MA.

We generated 11 buy signals over the October 2003 to December 31, 2007 time frame. We held stock for a total of 125 trading days (about 12 percent of the sample), and we saw returns, *not* counting interest earned in cash when we were out, of 11.42 percent.

Sounds pretty good, except that this is a total return over a time frame where the market returned 39.4 percent, and we had no stop of any sort to protect against a 2008-style disaster.

And if we tweak it a bit as shown in Table 9.1 and buy when the four-day PC gets 10 percent above the 20-day SMA, will the VIX 9 percent be above its 20-day SMA? Similar story—10.6 percent win total.

I imagine we could find an okay system here somewhere, but certainly nothing extraordinary.

## What About on an Individual Stock?

We have looked on a market level for meaning behind a mélange of put/call data. But what about on an individual stock? In other words, does a high put/call reading in say AAPL portend anything for AAPL specifically? And by AAPL I mean "proxy for any individual name with relatively active options."

On an anecdotal level, I would say no. Avoid most directional judgments when hearing about a big options print in a relatively popular name. This gets back to one of the original questions. How do we know whether this was a smart money player or not? And the answer is that we generally don't. A big put block going up in AAPL could mean smart money knowing that the new iPhone stopped selling, or he might simply be a nervous stock owner irrationally worried that the new iPhone is not selling. These have diametrically opposite implications for the stock, and you will really never know which, if either, is right. Or it may be none of the above.

On a more statistical level, there is not enormous correlation between an individual stock put/call and individual stock action. Schaeffer runs interesting data on put/call open-interest ratios. The chart in Figure 9.5 shows AAPL over the two-year stretch covering most of 2007 and 2008, compared with AAPL stock.

If anything, AAPL moves with the ratio more than against it. But then there's the chart shown in Figure 9.6, XOM, over the same time frame.

And it's a bit more as expected. High put/calls are more bullish; lows more bearish.

My point though isn't to parse these two charts, but rather to just show that Put/Call is not a great indicator for individual stock action

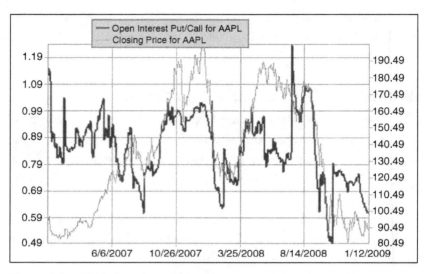

**Figure 9-5**    AAPL Open Interest Put/Call vs. AAPL Stock, 2007-2008 via
Schaeffer's Research

**Figure 9-6**    XOM Open Interest Put/Call vs. AAPL Stock, 2007-2008 via
Schaeffer's Research

in a big name. At best, it's a stat that works on the macro level, really not the micro level.

What about the same situation in a less active name? Maybe a different story. You have to give the "smart money" theory greater weight. Anecdotally again, I would assume that you want to go with the order flow until you're proven wrong. Keep in mind however, that an odd trade in a less active name hits every tape in about two minutes, so I'd classify this as a more "don't fight it" suggestion than a "jump on in."

## Summary

What a learning process for yours truly. I admit it. I totally did not believe I would find much value in the put/call ratio. We noted a host of reasons why a given trade may mislead.

I expected the ISEE improvements would prove better (wrong).

The put/call ratio basically oscillates, and we can guess where it goes next with some degree of accuracy. Yet this ability of prognostication does not translate into the ability to pick the market direction, which transitively implies that the put/call will not help us much. Yet it has some utility, especially when combined with a volatility indicator. Oddly though, an extreme high put/call and an extreme low put/call play out bullishly by different metrics.

System trades are perhaps a little more troublesome.

What I would do though is put this tool in the shed. I used 10, 15, and 20 percent extensions of the four-day put/call ratio versus the 20-day ratio and 8, 9 or 10 percent extensions of the VIX above the 20-day SMA and did find some indication that it boded well for the market when certain combos of the above took place.

As to individual stocks, I would steer clear of reading too much into isolated put/call quirks.

# Chapter 10

# WE'RE (PIN)
# JAMMIN'

We set the forces of good (calls) against the forces of evil (puts) against each other in Chapter 9. Why can't we all get along? As we get closer to expiration, the side of the trade becomes less and less significant, and what becomes more significant is a "long paper" and "short paper" discussion. And when we get to expiration, we think more and more about pinning.

Ah, pinning. That occurrence when a stock gets magnetized to a strike price on or near expiration and just sits there and can't move away. Sort of like the Millennium Falcon unable to escape the Death Star tractor beam in the first *Star Wars* movie.

The whole subject raises all sorts of questions—and no shortage of virulent opinion as to the answers.

Does pinning really happen, or do we just think we see it because we get attuned to it on expiration? In other words, do stocks close at strikes with any more frequency on expiration than, say, the second Tuesday of the month?

How does pinning happen? Real (and spectacular) or with some augmentation? And by augmentation, I mean manipulation. What backdrop might cause it to happen, and is it something we can anticipate?

If in fact it does happen, can we the investor-trader at worst avoid taking a profit hit for no reason on it, and at best make some coin playing for it?

Let's dig in and delve into some of these questions.


## Pinning at Strike. Urban Legend?

When I began my market-making career on the AMEX, here is how expiration day tended to work. If you had a stock about a buck or less above a strike price, you would spend the entire day buying expiring calls on that strike and then shorting stock against the calls you bought. Hopefully for a $1/8$- or a $1/16$-point profit. Over and over again. The stock would tend to have a permanent offer to it, likely part from our crowd selling every share in sight against the calls we keep buying.

The kicker in the trade? We have now accumulated synthetic puts for zero, or perhaps a credit. So a move below strike allows us to buy all that stock back, and in turn now ride free calls in case we U-turn and rally again.

But the trade never seems to generate that easy home run. It would get to strike then magically just stop. Yes, you likely scalped some change in the process, but that theoretical windfall proved elusive.

So color me a big believer that pins do in fact exist.

Statistical evidence does support the general belief that stocks do tend to pin at or near strike on expiration day, albeit not as frequently as the average observer or conspiracy theorist would surmise.

Neil D. Pearson and Allen M. Poteshman, finance professors at the University of Illinois Chicago, along with Ph.D. student Sophie Xiaoyan Ni, studied the topic and presented a paper titled "Stock Price Clustering on Options Expiration Dates" on August 27, 2004. Mark Hulbert wrote it up for the *New York Times* on May 7, 2004.

The researchers focused on unusual trading patterns of stocks when options on them were expiring. They found an increased likelihood that a stock would close on the options expiration day at or very near the strike price of one of its expiring options.

A strike price, of course, is the price at which an option's owner can buy the underlying stock (if the option is a call) or sell the stock (if the option is a put). A stock typically has options with many different strike prices, set at regular intervals — every $5, for example. Options also vary by month of expiration; all of a given month's options expire on the third Friday.

In effect, the researchers found that the closing prices of stocks that have options were not randomly distributed on expiration days, but instead tended to cluster around the strike prices of certain of their options.

Consider how often a stock closes within 12.5 cents of one of its option's strike prices. On all days other than the expiration date, the researchers found, this happens about 10.5 percent of the time. But on option expiration days, this frequency jumps a full percentage point, to around 11.5 percent. That suggests that option strike prices are acting like magnets, drawing stock prices toward them.

This clustering may not seem a big deal, but the researchers say they are confident that it can't be attributed to chance.

Yes, to the naked eye, the move from 10.5 percent to 11.5 percent does in fact not seem like a big deal. But statistically there's a near 10 percent increase in the likelihood of a pin.

And in the paper itself, the researchers make an excellent case that the increased likelihood does not occur by mere happenstance. The study period covers from 1996 to 2002. "Optionable" stocks cluster near strike to a greater degree than nonoptionable stocks. Stocks that became optionable over that stretch saw an increased likelihood of pinning once they became optionable. Stocks in reverse, with delisted options, became less likely to pin, although I would suggest that this finding may merely reflect that any stock that went in that direction would likely trade at a very low dollar amount. And strikes under $5 were not common at the time. Not to mention a very high volatility if they did exist.

But that's neither here nor there. Anecdotal experience and mathematical evidence reach similar conclusions; stocks do have an increased tendency to pin near expiration. So we will continue on the premise that clustering happens.

## How and Why Do We See Pins?

How and why do we see pins? There's pretty simple dynamic. On expiration day, options go "binary." They have either a 100 delta or a 0. Or in English, they become 100 shares of stock long or short, or they expire worthless. Consider a call with a strike a shade below where the stock trades. Say that the call has a near 50 delta, meaning that every call holder owns the equivalent of about 50 shares of stock per call. Now it's expiration day. If the stock closes above strike, that will translate to the call holder owning 100 shares of stock per call. She possibly has shorted stock against it already, and possibly not.

In any case, she most certainly has to take some action. Either offer stock for sale against the calls she owns or just offer to sell the calls outright. Multiply this player by an entire marketplace, and you have excess pressure on the stock on the margins.

But that pressure only exists down to the strike price. Once it goes below, the call now has 0 delta. In fact that call holder who shorted stock against her calls now actually has a bearish position working should it close below strike. So she can actually buy stock below strike. And ergo we now have a bid on the margins at lower prices.

What's the net effect of bids below a strike and offers above a strike, possibly from the same actual players?

Well, they are forces for a pin, on the margins.

Now of course we have a simple case here. We have not considered puts. Or the fact that options are a zero sum game. For each owner we have a short that has the desire to get the stock near strike. But the risk that if the stock is running away from strike, he may have to chase strength and/or fade weakness and add a small force that contributes to moving the stock against his wishes.

As to the puts, well it's similar to the call dynamic above, at least in terms of the long side. A put owner has the ammo to buy stock below strike. Then if she owns stock versus her put holding, she has the ammo to sell that stock back out above strike. So options owners really have the same motivations and interests regardless of whether they own puts or calls.

So we really must look at this more as net option owners versus net option sellers. Net owners want everything as far from strikes they own as possible. For net sellers, it's the reverse.

Who wins?

To borrow a little Seinfeld, whoever has the upper "hand" wins. If shorts have "hand," we see longs scrambling to salvage those precious last vestiges of time decay, likely in the manner we just discussed; selling stock above strike and buying stock below strike and in a way causing their own self-fulfilling prophecy of a pin. Shorts have the wind at their backs as the stock looks headed for strike, and they will likely bide their time and do little or nothing. They'll just let the position sort itself out.

If longs have hand, quite the opposite is the case. Options shorts must run for cover as the stock moves away from strike. And to flatten out, the longs must chase strength and short weakness.

## About That Hand

Several factors come into play regarding whether a pin looks likely or not, and who is the favorite to get that hand. We're talking about a pin at least somewhere near where the stock trades now.

Open interest, who holds that open interest, how (really when) that open interest formed, volatility of the stock itself, and general market volatility all play a role.

Open interest is almost self-explanatory—to a point. The greater the open interest, the more likely a stock will pin. On the surface. Remember, options are just one force affecting a stock price. So if we have boatloads of calls outstanding relative to typical volume in the stock, it stands to reason that we will have more natural stock sellers hedging those calls. And then more stock to buy below strike. And so on.

But it's not quite so simple. It matters in whose hands that open interest lies. I mean actual hands, not metaphorical ones.

Floor market makers (MMs), specialists, and professional trading desks (often one and resume) represent far and away the most likely parties to hedge option-related deltas aggressively. This is pretty much modus operandi for a business model that essentially attempts to collect spreads and ride order flow for a living. Risking too much in the way of deltas tends to defeat any advantage trading order flow might confer. Thus the greater the percentage of calls the professionals own, the more likely they get in there, sit on the stock, and get it near a strike.

And the timing of when they acquired that open interest may have an effect too. The later in the cycle it came about, the more likely the pin. At least that's the finding from the aforementioned study. And that logically makes sense as we show later in this chapter. The later the trade, the more intense the hedging nearer to expiry vis-à-vis a more stale position that suddenly gets near the money and in play and was likely hedged long ago.

Of course the reverse holds true as well. If professionals short near money calls, the stock may work against a pin because that disciplined hedging may become self-defeating, though only to a degree since it's important to note that a long and a short do not exactly mirror each other. Time decay will always put the wind at the short's back, so in effect a stock needs energy to get away from a strike, as opposed to inertia to stay near to it. Think escape velocity of a rocket ship breaking out of earth's atmosphere.

Which segues neatly into our next factor—volatility.

Volatility *is* a proxy for that very escape velocity. Low volatility implies a low expected range for a stock on any given day, which logically implies that it won't get very far from where you see it right now no matter what day in the cycle it is. Under such circumstances, option open interest has a greater impact on the stock price. And likely a negative one, or at least one where the greatest energy out there involves panic-stricken call owners flipping stock as fervently as they can. And that strike price serves as gravity.

In the reverse case, the rocket has moved fast enough to escape earth's gravitational pull. Elvis has left the building. Or, if you prefer clarity of language, the stock has moved away from strike.

High volatility implies a large range, which implies that the larger option force will involve options shorts scrambling to avert a complete squeeze. And those shorts will self-defeat as they chase/pound the stock and increase that very volatility they must defend against. And the more strikes the stock threatens or busts through, the more shorts get squeezed and the more volatility increases. That same 0 or 100 delta nature of every option on expiration day that works to option shorts' favor on slow days works to their detriment on expiration days. Exponentially so. Remember that options owners can lose only what they spent on the option, while shorts have theoretically limitless exposure.

And in this setup—options longs with hand—higher open interest actually makes a stock less likely to pin.

It's important to note that this happens with less frequency than a long squeeze, but given the asymmetric risks of the two, causes exponentially more pain to the losing side.

## Can We Anticipate Pins or Squeezes?

To some extent, we can anticipate pins or squeezes, though I would classify this as more art than science. We have no magical formula that says, "When open interest as a percent of daily volume equals X, and volatility equals Y, then a pin will happen at strike price Z.

There are several questions we must answer:

- *Is the market backdrop volatile now?* Remember, a pin force exists strictly on the margins. Any real stock-specific or market-specific news will trump it in a heartbeat. Exxon won't magically ignore a market melt or oil boom or earnings reaction or whatever just to move near a strike with high open interest.
- *Is the stock itself volatile?* Same principal as above. A wildly fluctuating stock may very well pin somewhere, but who knows what strike? We've seen GOOG as a frequent pin candidate, yet it's often 30–40 points away from where it started. What's the tradable edge there? You guessed it—nothing.
- *Do the market makers net own the options?* This is clearly something that we need to infer. But fear not. We can actually infer it. The default setting is that MMs do in fact own most of the call open interest by the very nature of their trading existence. They take the opposite side of public order flow, and public order flow overwhelmingly sells calls, as buy-writing far and away represents the most common options play out there. So all things being

equal, it pays to assume that MMs own the calls. *What would make things not equal?* Well, a lift in implied volatility over the course of an expiration cycle. Implied volatility generally moves flat to down, unless the public order flow net buys it. In which case MMs are likely to simultaneously short options, lifting their bids and offers to get better pricing on the next batch of sales.

- *What accounts for the importance of whose hands the long side of the open interest resides?* The fact that market makers serve as far and away the most aggressive delta hedgers in the pond. We presume that they keep their positions in line at most times and thus stand to have the most inclination to remain that way as expiration nears and gamma lifts and adjustments get tighter and trickier.

## What a Cycle Might Look Like

Basically, an expiration cycle will have a personality. One of strong and/or increasing volatility heading into expiration week, say something like October 2008, shown in Figure 10.1 with a two measures of volatility (average true range and Bollinger band width).

Guess what? Increasing volatility over the course of the cycle snowballed into a frenzy on expiration week as the SPY saw two days of near 10 percent moves.

That's quite extreme and probably not repeatable. But by the same token, playing for pins the last week of an already nutty expiration cycle will prove hazardous for your financial health about 100 percent of the time.

Want to see the flipside? You had to wait all of two cycles. Figure 10.2 shows December 2008.

You could barely detect a pulse on expiration week as SPY fluctuated between 88 and low 90 for pretty much the entirety of the final four days. It's pretty safe to say that when you see broad measures of

**Figure 10-1** SPY Bollinger Band Width and Average True Range, October Expiration Cycle 2008, via StockCharts.com

volatility taking a nosedive into expiration week, you won't see much volatility on actual expiration week, which of course should give you some inkling that you should at least sift through your portfolio and find some pin candidates. And at most, hunt for some new positions that may pin.

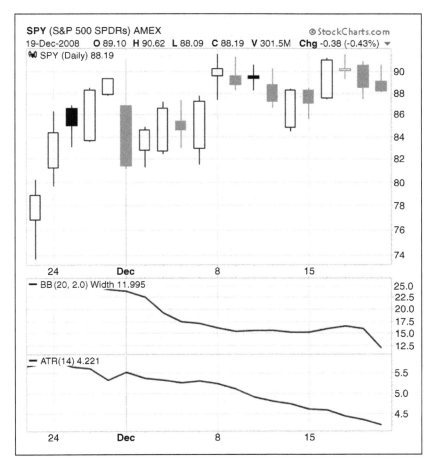

**Figure 10-2**   SPY Bollinger Band Width and Average True Range, December Expiration Cycle 2008, via StockCharts.com

## So When Should I Start Looking?

You're probably wondering when you should start looking for a pin? On the one hand, if you sit in a cycle, as discussed above, with cascading options premiums, proactive pays off as far as pins go. But stay realistic and don't go nuts with anticipation. Remember always, pinning just exerts a force on the margins; it's no be-all and end-all. The numbers just don't add up sometimes.

Let's take a hypothetical stock XYZ. Say the stock trades at 71, while the 70 line calls have a sizable open interest. Let's call it 20,000 versus typical daily volume of 5 million shares. That's a relatively high ratio of open interest to average volume. Using a 40 volatility, these calls have a .6285 delta at the start of trading on Monday.

Now let's assume that market makers own the entire open interest, the best possible hands if you root for a pin at 70. Let's also assume that, as the most aggressive delta hedgers in the pool, the market makers were flat delta entering the week, so they are already short 1,257,000 shares or share equivalents compared to the calls they own. And then they flatten out each day by shorting more stock as needed. And we'll assume that the puts have no open interest and that the call shorts take no action over the course of the week.

And finally we'll assume that the stock closes at 71 each day as we're trying to isolate the incremental selling pressure on the shares.

Table 10.1 shows how much extra stock we can expect on the offer each day under these conditions.

It's pretty clear from the numbers in the table that natural pin pressure early in a week borders on the nonexistent, whereas by Friday it

**Table 10-1**  Hypothetical Delta Neutral Hedge Quantity

| Day | Option Delta at Close | Extra Stock for Sale |
| --- | --- | --- |
| Monday | .6409 | 24,800 |
| Tuesday | .6592 | 36,600 |
| Wednesday | .6896 | 60,800 |
| Thursday | .7545 | 129,800 |
| Friday | 1.000 | 491,000 |

can reach nearly 10 percent of the typical daily volume. So basically leave the gaming of pins early in an expiration week to financial pundits who throw out these calls with nary a wisp of analysis.

By Friday though, we have some real pressure building up. Of course some will anticipate and short early, so the actual distribution will show a more even split.

But still.

This includes only one side of the trade—the natural sellers. Option shorts may have the wind at their backs, but they will presumably take some action along the way, particularly if the stock moves away from strike early in the week as they may get forced to chase. So the numbers in the table represent maxed-out imbalances.

Just to use one real-life example, I examined XOM options on expiration week of the December cycle in 2006. The stock at the time sat a bit above the 75 strike. And XOM is a big and not terribly volatile stock in what at the time was a very tame and nonvolatile market. An ideal time and place for a drift to a pin over the course of expiration week.

XOM Dec 75 calls had an open interest of 18,346 entering that Monday. They had a delta of about 60. And again, let's assume that market makers own all of them, and they aggressively hedge to the extent that they are "delta neutral" at the close of every day.

This would mean that they were already short 1,100,760 shares against them and would have (1,834,600 − 1,100,760), or 733,840 shares left *total* of XOM to sell between Monday and Friday. In a stock that had traded 6.7 million shares in half a day Monday.

Using the same sort of pattern as in Table 10.1, you can see that the stock for sale early in the week when the pin was called was pretty much nonexistent. Later in the week, the stock had lifted to 80. And that relatively small quantity of stock presumed for sale in a pin at 75 actually had to chase and buy it into 80, no doubt some of which was offered by happy owners of the 75 line. Even the ones that were flattening each day.

Of course the earlier in the week you game a pin, the better the profits for the simple reason that premiums decline as the week goes on. The problem is that the chances of a pin at that point are pretty random. In reality, your best chance is when volatility is on the low end, which of course means lower premiums for taking the risk but better odds of success.

Bottom line though, patience makes the most sense of all. I'd rather wait until Thursday and have a feel for the week and a feel for the stock before I gamed it. Let someone else roll the dice earlier; the odds do not favor her.

## What If Someone Rigs the Game?

Someone may rig the game for himself. By this I mean that an options short sits on the stock with all sorts of offers and creates his own pin. The authors of the study mentioned earlier in the chapter, serial wolf-spotter Jim Cramer, and many others, suspect that this happens routinely. Options shorts ganging up on the underlying shares and pushing them near strike, causing the option longs to get into the self-defeating flip-around-the-strike cycle.

Does it happen? I have no way of knowing. But I suspect that if it does, it's a relatively minor force. The numbers make it look unlikely.

Take the above hypothetical XYZ example. Suppose one party holds the entire options short, all 20,000 contracts. They have a value of $1.87 on Monday, meaning she stands to gain a total of $3.74 million if the calls all go worthless. So she wants to short stock to make that pin become reality. But how much stock would do the trick? This thing trades 5 million shares per day without her. She might have to short 500,000 or 1 million shares to get it going there. But if she does that, she's going to generate a natural buyer; the call owner who can now buy some stock back as it gets cheaper. So she may have to short even more stock as it gets lower, which of course puts her at real risk if the stock turns and rallies in her face for whatever reason. And it's a real double risk since she's piling onto calls she's already short.

So while I could never prove options shorts don't pile on, color me skeptical. And let me so note that unless someone can prove an option short has set out to manipulate a stock by shorting it, this person has done nothing illegal while taking a huge risk shorting the stock.

But I find these points red herrings to begin with. We know anecdotally, and historically, that stocks do pin. Our job involves finding them, not blaming them on someone. We have enough natural factors to guide us here; we don't need to waste time speculating about unnatural ones.

No one has the ability to create a pin out of the ether. He can compound his risk and maybe make one more likely. That's about it.

## Maximum Pain

Do options drive stocks to a max pain spot, a place where long premium net-net does its worst? To a point, sure. The market itself really is a max pain being. I mean, to paraphrase from Jesse Livermore, the market always wants to go higher with the fewest participants possible and lower with everybody onboard. Options fit into that whole ecosystem. If max pain in the general sense involves a stock going to a certain price, and options have something to do with that, then sure, one can say that the stock moved to the max pain spot.

But max pain can work only so far. And it doesn't necessarily mean it pins. A stock won't jump through three strikes on its own to expire at a strike with the highest open interest.

Remember first of all that if a stock sits nowhere near that strike, longs and shorts there have likely long ago adjusted their positions accordingly. Take the above XYZ again. Let's say that instead of 71, XYZ sits near 80 with a week to go, while 70 remains the strike with the largest open interest and remains the theoretical max pain spot. Owners of the 70s have likely sold stock 1:1 against them, while shorts probably bought most or all of their stock back. Now let's say the stock and/or market has gotten plowed such that the 70 line is in play again. I would suggest far from max pain drawing the stock to a pin, it's quite the opposite. The call shorts suddenly have a synthetic put short on that they probably forgot about. But now it needs tending to of the stock selling variety. Longs meanwhile have a windfall out of the blue, as the synthetic puts that seemed worthless a day ago now have real value.

Easy to see who has "hand." And who faces max pain: the options shorts. They likely serve to drive the stock *away* from 70.

So yes I believe in max pain—very much so. I believe it's lazy and quite dangerous logic to believe that max pain implies that a stock will get drawn to a big open interest strike in a vacuum. It's just not that simple in real trading life.

## Summary

Pins do happen. I have lived through many. Statistical data appear to back up that notion.

The higher the volatility, the less likely the stock will pin. And in fact, I would consider the general volatility backdrop as the single most important factor in predicting pin likelihood, at least a pin at a nearby strike.

Higher open interest can predict a pin, but only to a point. It depends on how and when that open interest formed, who has the long side, and whether it is calls or puts.

The greater the percentage of calls owned by professionals and the later in the cycle they bought it, the more likely we see a pin.

Higher open interest works in reverse in an increasing volatility environment. If options shorts must scramble, it's very probable that the stock does anything *but* pin, at least at a strike that the shorts want to see.

Last thing I would worry about is a manipulated pin. Even if you believe that manipulated pins do happen, no one is big enough to generate a pin on his own. If someone causes one, the seeds were probably there already.

And most of all, don't anticipate. The forces are so small early in the week that patience makes the most sense of all.

# Chapter 11

# MYTH-BUSTING AND OTHER ASSORTED OPTIONS- AND EXPIRATION- RELATED STATS

We certainly have no shortage of rules and aphorisms and guidelines when it comes to pins as we saw in Chapter 10. Not to mention the VIX and volatility in general as we have noted throughout the book. Let's actually examine a few of these with some relatively simple statistical analyses. We'll see what's real and what's a bit of a tall tale.

## Expiration Day—Great Volatility or Greatest Volatility?

Does expiration day provide great volatility or the greatest volatility? The answer? Neither.

Turn on the TV around expiration day, and you find all sorts of dire warnings. Stay inside. Load up on duct tape and canned food. Whatever you do, tread carefully lest that volatility carry you away. Many a day trader takes the day off. In fact, all that actually makes some sense because, if nothing else, we see a *different* sort of action. And general rules may not work to the extent that they normally do.

But is the day actually more volatile? Evidence seems to suggest a big no.

Let's take a closer look. We took each day from May 1988 to the end of 2007 and labeled it by where it sat in the expiration cycle. Day 1 is expiration day, Day 2 is Thursday of expiration week, and so on. We calculated the natural log (LN) of each day as part of an HV formula, and then stacked all those LNs for each Day 1, Day 2, and so on as if they were consecutive days. And we then calculated a historical volatility for each day of the cycle.

This is not a measurement I would rely on for trading per se because historical volatility should measure a continuous time stretch and not an artificially concocted one. But nevertheless it does give a general picture. If expiration days were more volatile than others, it would show up here.

So let's rank each day from most to least volatile. (See Table 11.1.) As you can see, we get a bit of a mishmash. The early cycle days tend toward lesser volatility. Barely.

And expiration day? It's right smack dab in the middle of the chart—pretty much nothing.

In the trading world, expiration day feels like it does everything to the extreme. A volatile expiration day seems extra volatile, and a slow one seems particularly soporific. But the numbers suggest that it's just a normal day.

**Table 11-1** Realized Volatility by Day in Expiration Cycle

| Day | HV |
| --- | --- |
| 6 | 17.66819 |
| 14 | 17.59418 |
| 20 | 17.37505 |
| 15 | 17.3057 |
| 11 | 16.63654 |
| 7 | 16.5709 |
| 2 | 16.1217 |
| 19 | 15.85539 |
| 23 | 15.76606 |
| 4 | 15.68647 |
| 7 | 15.60639 |
| 17 | 15.2836 |
| 1 | 15.17895 |
| 8 | 15.00804 |
| 9 | 14.95936 |
| 25 | 14.8915 |
| 21 | 14.83561 |
| 22 | 14.83114 |
| 18 | 14.75325 |
| 12 | 14.27991 |
| 3 | 14.27315 |
| 10 | 14.26493 |
| 24 | 14.10229 |
| 13 | 13.8134 |
| 16 | 13.05911 |

## Does Expiration Week See the Greatest Volatility in the Cycle?

If you're wondering whether expiration week sees the greatest volatility in the cycle, you can stop wondering. The answer is yes, it does.

This question may require the equivalent of standing on one leg and holding one of those old TVs with the rabbit ears in order to get reception. I fully understand that anyone born after something like 1980 has probably never seen a TV with rabbit ears. But just play along with me.

I jiggered a formula for historical volatility to pretend that weeks were just days, and then I analyzed the "overnight" (really one week) performances for every week from May 1988 to the end of December 2007. So I created a 52-day year for the 252-trading-day year that we normally use.

These volatility readings are not perfectly comparable to normal historical volatility readings. But they are comparable to one another.

And here's what we came up with: Week 1 is expiration week; Week 2, the week before; and so on. Week 4 is the first week of the expiration cycle about two-thirds of the time, and the second week of the cycle the other third of the time. (See Table 11.2.)

**Table 11-2**  Realized Volatility by Week in Cycle

| Week of Cycle | Volatility |
| --- | --- |
| Week 1 (expiration) | 15.11159 |
| Week 2 | 13.62931 |
| Week 3 | 13.16807 |
| Week 4 | 13.39501 |
| Week 5 | 13.28338 |

And indeed by this metric, Week 1 shows more volatility than any other week in the cycle. In fact the other four weeks bunch up, while Week 1 really stands out.

On the surface, this seems to contradict findings from Chapter 5 (Volatility Timing) and the first question in this chapter where we showed that HV segmented by day of the cycle did not show any particular volatility on days from expiration week. But they actually measure something different—day-to-day moves. Perhaps these day-to-day moves tend to offset each other to a greater extent on nonexpiration weeks than they do on expiration weeks. If that's the case, then we should expect to see less randomness from day to day on expiration week than we see on days outside expiration week.

In other words, the volatility of a full week taken as a unit unto itself depends on both the volatility of the days comprising the week and the degree to which those days correlate (move in the same direction). If the correlation is greater for days on expiration week than it is for days not on expiration week, then we can in fact see increased volatility for expiration week taken as a whole.

So is the correlation positive, and greater, on expiration week than at other times?

Sort of. We examined the correlation of each individual day of the expiration cycle compared to the day prior to it. If a day has no memory, it will have close to zero correlation. Highest positive means that this particular day in the cycle has tended to follow the prior day the most, highest negative means that it has tended to move in opposition.

Table 11.3 presents each day, labeled by number (Day 1 again being expiration), and ranked from highest correlation to lowest.

There's a modestly higher bias to positive correlation early and late in the expiration cycle. Expiration day itself and the day just pre-

Table 11-3  Correlation to Prior Session By Day of Expiration Cycle

| | |
|---|---|
| Day 23 | .168298 |
| Day 20 | .149584 |
| Day 2 | .136129 |
| Day 1 | .126508 |
| Day 15 | .101496 |
| Day 10 | .098195 |
| Day 5 | .073663 |
| Day 11 | .066281 |
| Day 22 | .05619 |
| Day 12 | .037562 |
| Day 17 | .003194 |
| Day 16 | −.00329 |
| Day 7 | −.01991 |
| Day 6 | −.02613 |
| Day 14 | −.0346 |
| Day 3 | −.059 |
| Day 8 | −.06371 |
| Day 24 | −.09395 |
| Day 9 | −.11677 |
| Day 19 | −.14084 |
| Day 4 | −.17936 |
| Day 13 | −.17936 |
| Day 25 | −.18723 |
| Day 21 | −.20517 |
| Day 18 | −.21834 |

ceding it are easily the most powerful two-day trending combo in the cycle. But you also get a very negative correlation day thrown in—the Tuesday of expiration week.

So basically the data here tells me not to fight the trend established on Wednesday of expiration week.

And a couple of other interesting points jump out. Day 13 and Day 18 are both early-cycle Wednesdays. And both show extreme negative correlation to the day prior. Let's keep that in mind as we make our next bold statement.

## Expiration Week Tends to Be Strong; Post-Expiration Tends to Be Weak

Does expiration week tend to be strong and post-expiration tend to be weak? Answer? Basically yes.

We looked at each day in the cycle from May 1988 to December 31, 2007, and analyzed and ranked them on a simple won-lost basis. The results are shown in Table 11.4.

All five days from expiration week rank in the top nine in terms of win percentage. Day 4 is kind of odd, given that, as we see in Table 11.4, it tends pretty strongly to move in opposition to Day 5. What we apparently see with some regularity is two offsetting days on Monday and Tuesday of expiration week (turnaround Tuesday anyone?) followed by a pretty good chance of consistent strength for the remainder of the week.

Two other days stand out—Days 13 and 18. Again, two nondescript Wednesdays. And for that we have little explanation. Just something to make note of.

## There Really Is Such a Thing as Turnaround Tuesday

Is there such a thing as turnaround Tuesday? Yes, there is. At least there is if you believe the correlation numbers from Table 11.4.

The theory states that we tend to see turnarounds on Tuesdays. These are reversals of the previous day's move.

**Table 11-4** Won-Loss Record by Day in Expiration Cycle

|         | Wins | Losses | Win %     |
|---------|------|--------|-----------|
| Day 5   | 141  | 82     | 63.22877% |
| Day 13  | 137  | 91     | 60.00877% |
| Day 18  | 138  | 93     | 59.7403%  |
| Day 10  | 127  | 90     | 58.5253%  |
| Day 6   | 132  | 94     | 58.4071%  |
| Day 1   | 133  | 102    | 56.5957%  |
| Day 2   | 132  | 103    | 56.1702%  |
| Day 3   | 131  | 104    | 55.7447%  |
| Day 4   | 129  | 106    | 54.8936%  |
| Day 11  | 122  | 103    | 54.2222%  |
| Day 23  | 44   | 38     | 53.6585%  |
| Day 14  | 121  | 106    | 53.304%   |
| Day 19  | 121  | 109    | 52.6087%  |
| Day 15  | 119  | 113    | 51.2931%  |
| Day 17  | 110  | 106    | 50.9259%  |
| Day 16  | 116  | 113    | 50.655%   |
| Day 12  | 114  | 115    | 49.7179%  |
| Day 21  | 38   | 40     | 48.7179%  |
| Day 7   | 113  | 121    | 48.2906%  |
| Day 8   | 112  | 122    | 47.8632%  |
| Day 22  | 37   | 42     | 46.8354%  |
| Day 25  | 36   | 41     | 46.7532%  |
| Day 24  | 38   | 44     | 46.3415%  |
| Day 9   | 102  | 132    | 43.5897%  |
| Day 20  | 89   | 118    | 42.9952%  |

Tuesdays in the cycle on the system in Table 11.4 are Days 4, 9, 14, 19, and 24. And they see correlations of −.17936, −.11677, −.0346, −.14084, and −.09395, respectively, with the move from the day before. And these are all negative.

## The Thursday in the Week before Expiration Moves in Opposition to the Expiration Direction

Does the Thursday in the week before expiration move in opposition to the expiration direction? No, it doesn't.

Ah, the Legend of Misdirection Thursday.

As we are told, whichever way the market goes on the Thursday before expiration is the opposite of the direction it will move in expiration week. My friend Rob Hanna of the Quantifiable Edges blog ran the data, and here's what came back:

> Buying (shorting) at the close on Thursday before expiration week if the market was down (up) and selling (covering) the Friday of expirations would have netted the following results since July 1978:
> Trades—354
> Winners—171
> Losers—182 (1 breakeven)
> Average trade—0.08%

In an unrelated story, coin flips and darts outperformed this one.

What about if we just refine the rule to say that misdirection Thursday moves in opposition to expiration Friday? This doesn't really do much for us. Misdirection Thursday has a –.10697 correlation to expiration Friday. That's not a lot to trade on, but it does lead to the question, Is there a day out there that does in fact move in opposition to expiration?

We looked at some other nearby days. The Friday one week before expiration day has a .100106 correlation to the expiration day move. The next trading day, expiration week Monday, has a .083344 correlation, while the next day, Tuesday, has a .026597 correlation.

So there's wisp of sense in the original statement. Misdirection Thursday bears little relevance to the next six trading days in sum total, but it does have a modest inverse relationship to expiration day itself.

## Expiration Really Extends Another Day of Trading

Does expiration really extend another day of trading (kind of like an options version of a hangover)? No, it doesn't.

Not all positions get resolved on expiration day. I mean beyond cash settled options, which by definition, settle. So common sense says that we see some follow-through to whatever trend was in place on expiration day. But if that's the case, we find scant statistical evidence of it.

For the purposes of this experiment, we will isolate the first day of each expiration cycle from the same 1988–2007 sample and group them as one, regardless of the length of the cycle, whether it started on a Tuesday, or whatever. Then we will measure correlation to the market move on both expiration day and expiration week. And we find it as disconnected as any random pair. The first day post expiration has a mere .019912 correlation to expiration day. And it has a .003378 correlation to expiration week as a whole.

So while we do see evidence of a post-expiration hangover as far as volatility (or lack thereof) is concerned, we don't see any real relationship to what happened the week or day before; it's a new leaf, a new universe, each time the cycle changes.

## It's a Warning Signal if the VIX Does Not Do What It Is "Supposed" to Do

If the VIX doesn't do what it's supposed to do, is that a big warning signal? The answer is both yes and no.

If you see the market collapsing, what do you expect to see as far as volatility is concerned?

This is not a trick question. We expect to see the VIX explode. Over the same two-decade time frame, the VIX has a −.67308 correlation to the SPX. That's about what we would reasonably expect.

So we looked at outlier days, days where the SPX declined by over 1.5 percent on the day.

There were 263 separate instances. On those days, the median move in the VIX was an 8.5769 percent lift. So we will call that an equilibrium of some sort. And then we will ask, What does the SPX do when the VIX underperforms (rises less than 8.5769 percent), and what does it do when it overperforms? We will stipulate that observations must be at least five days apart so as to somewhat avoid double-counting, and then we will measure the mean and median returns over the next 5, 15 and 30 days. (See Table 11.5.)

The results shown in Table 11.5 are truly unspectacular. Returns are good all over the board. On a median basis, returns are slightly better in the high-volatility setup than in the low one. But there's hardly enough to read much into it. The third column simply measures market performance regardless of VIX. And again the information shows small outperformance after sell-offs with higher VIXs, but not much. And remember, none of this includes 2008, a year where getting long at strong VIX readings proved disastrous.

**Table 11-5**  Mean and Median SPY Returns on Above/Below Normal VIX Performance

| SPX Down 1.5% | VIX Up Above Average | VIX Up Less Than Average | Any VIX |
|---|---|---|---|
| Observations | 85 | 84 | 172 |
| Average 5-day return | .3181% | .4993% | .3574% |
| Median 5-day return | .5781% | .4555% | .4555% |
| Average 15-day return | .7209% | .8686% | .6884% |
| Median 15-day return | 1.2930% | 1.1608% | 1.0804% |
| Average 30-day return | 1.4893% | 2.004% | 1.6105% |
| Median 30-day return | 2.5443% | 2.3399% | 2.35% |

But the information in the table divides into two VIX halves. What if instead we look for extremes? We find 524 instances of SPX declining by 1 percent in a day. For extreme panic, we'll look at days where the VIX lifted by more than 15 percent on the day of the 1 percent dip. And for extreme indifference, how about VIX up by less than 2 percent? And again, there's only one observation per week so as not to double and triple count. We'll also look at performance when we simply ignore the VIX.

At the extremes, we do see outperformance over 15- and 30-day time frames when volatility gets a bit panic-stricken, particularly on a median basis. And buying when volatility spikes does modestly outperform simply buying any time the market dips 1 percent.

What about the flip side—volatility on large up days? Generally speaking, high volatility (panic) is considered a better market tell than low volatility (complacency). So one could reasonably expect underwhelming performance here. And one would be wrong with that assumption. We looked at markets closing up 1.5 percent or more on the day, something that happened 253 times in the same old time frame we've used all chapter. Volatility generally dips on those days,

**Table 11-6**

| SPX Down 1% | VIX Up >15% | VIX Up < 2% | Any VIX |
|---|---|---|---|
| Observations | 53 | 49 | 312 |
| Average 5-day return | .3427% | .3524% | .3714% |
| Median 5-day return | .3025% | .1795% | .3334% |
| Average 15-day return | .8815% | .2949% | .7596% |
| Median 15-day return | 1.4302% | .9679% | 1.106% |
| Average 30-day return | 1.6382% | .1775% | 1.421% |
| Median 30-day return | 2.3808% | .5387% | 1.6927% |

so we considered extreme lows as dips greater than 11 percent in the VIX and extreme highs as dips under 2 percent. (See Table 11.7.)

Unusually strong VIX performance after a 1.5 percent (or greater) up day bodes well for the market 30 days out. Both when compared with any VIX, and particularly so when compared with a weak VIX. This actually makes sense if you believe in the VIX and believe that if the VIX holds up well in the face of a strong market, then there's too much fear around.

We don't see the same effect in the shorter time frames however, so it's kind of a mixed bag.

I could play with more numbers and tweak my trigger points, but I think we have some evidence here that improper VIX action does matter when you start going out in time. An unusually strong VIX does bode well for the market if you look in certain spots.

**Table 11-7**  Mean and Median SPY Returns on Extreme VIX Moves

| SPX Up 1.5% | VIX Up > –2% | VIX Up < –11% | Any VIX |
|---|---|---|---|
| Observations | 40 | 40 | 181 |
| Average 5-day return | .164% | .0273% | .4291% |
| Median 5-day return | .5400% | -.1097% | .3687% |
| Average 15-day return | .6017% | .8869% | .8461% |
| Median 15-day return | .7909% | .781% | .8892% |
| Average 30-day return | 2.767% | 1.7432% | 1.7596% |
| Median 30-day return | 3.7406% | 1.4455% | 2.2619% |

## Summary

So what have we learned?

We have all sorts of options and expiration-related "truths" we just take for granted. Some in fact are true. We do see more volatility in expiration week than in other weeks. But that's only if you look at the week as a whole, and it's thanks to a propensity for trending from day to day that is modestly larger than that propensity in other weeks.

Intraday volatility in expiration week is unexceptional. And as to follow-through? Expiration hangover? Not so much.

Misdirection Thursday? A bit of an urban legend. There is a small tendency for Misdirection Thursday to move in opposition to Expiration Friday, but there is no notable relationship between Misdirection Thursday and expiration week as a whole.

As to the VIX, we examined whether "odd" behavior tells us much of anything. And in fact it does, just not necessarily today or tomorrow or even by week's end. But if you hit a patch where you see a VIX too strong for a given market backdrop, it does appear to suggest too much fear in the marketplace, and this bodes well for the bulls three weeks and a month out.

# Chapter 12

# BUY-WRITE—
# YOU BET

W e've learned an awful lot about buying and selling volatility in the last few chapters. Now it's time to apply that knowledge to some actual options plays.

Buy-write; covered write; buy stock and sell a call against it; get the exposure of a naked put sale, but make it sound safe—whatever you want to call it. All these expressions refer to the same strategy, and it's far and away the most popular strategy that involves use of an option. There is no close second.

And it's seductive. Sell a call against a stock long, and you can essentially create your own dividend. And over time, you can approximate the returns of plain vanilla stock ownership, but with reduced volatility.

It sounds strange, but it's true. Selling a call, a sale of volatility, actually reduces the volatility of a portfolio.

In fact, so popular has the strategy been over the years, that the CBOE created an index in 2002 expressly to track a buy-write on the S&P 500 (SPX) under the symbol "BXM". Here's the CBOE press release announcing BXM:

The BXM is a benchmark index that measures potential returns of a theoretical portfolio of Standard & Poor's 500 Index stocks that also systematically sells S&P 500 Index call options (SPX) against the portfolio.

A "buy-write," also called a covered call, generally is considered to be an investment strategy in which an investor buys a stock or a basket of stocks, and also sells call options that correspond to the stock or basket of stocks. This strategy can be used to enhance portfolio returns and reduce volatility.

The BXM is a passive total return index based on selling the near-term, at-the-money S&P 500 Index (SPX) call option against the S&P 500 stock index portfolio each month, on the day the current contract expires. The SPX call that is sold (or written) will have one month remaining to expiration, with an exercise price just above the prevailing index level (i.e., slightly out-of-the-money). The premium collected from the sale of the call is added to the portfolio's total value. The SPX call is held until its expiration, at which time a new one-month, at-the-money call is written. The expired option, if exercised, is settled in cash.

CBOE developed the BXM in response to customer demand for a quantified performance measure of the buy-write strategy. Historical values for the BXM were calculated by CBOE and are available dating back to June 1988. Comparisons of the BXM to the S&P 500 Total Return Index also are available.

"For more than 25 years, portfolio managers have employed buy-write strategies to provide incremental income to boost risk-adjusted returns and provide a cushion against downside losses," said CBOE Chairman and CEO William J. Brodsky. "BXM is exactly the tool every money manager needs to measure the performance of these portfolios and compare buy-write portfolio performance to other benchmark indexes."

"The CBOE BuyWrite Monthly Index not only provides the first objective benchmark with which to assess managed buy-write fund performance but also serves to illustrate the risk/return management properties of hedged equity strategies in general," said Professor of Finance Robert Whaley. Whaley is professor of finance at the Fuqua School of Business at Duke University, and was instrumental in the development of the BXM. Whaley is also known for his work on the creation of CBOE's volatility indexes, VIX and VXN.

The new index is calculated and disseminated under the symbol "BXM," on a daily basis, using closing prices of the S&P 500 Index and the closing price of the selected SPX call.

And the index performed pretty much as expected. At least in hindsight. The CBOE provided data on its methodology back to June 1988. Consulting firm Ibbotson Associates studied the data in September 2004, and concluded this:

The results showed that the BXM Index has had relatively good risk-adjusted returns. The compound annual return of the BXM Index over the almost 16-year history of this study is 12.39 percent, compared to 12.20 percent for the S&P 500. The BXM had about two-thirds the volatility of the S&P 500. Risk-adjusted performance, as measured by the Stutzer index, was 0.22 for the BXM vs. 0.16 for the S&P 500. The study also found that the low tracking error (1.27 percent/yr) of the Rampart investable version of the BXM provides credible evidence of the investability of the BXM Index.

This was followed by a study by Callan Associates in 2006 that yielded similar results.

- BXM generated superior risk-adjusted returns over the last 18 years, generating a return comparable to that of the S&P 500 with approximately two-thirds of the risk. (The compound annual return of the BXM was 11.77% compared to 11.67% for the S&P 500, and BXM returns were generated with a standard deviation of 9.29%, two-thirds of the 13.89% volatility of the S&P 500.)
- The risk-adjusted performance, as measured by the monthly Stutzer Index over the 18-year period, was 0.20 for the BXM vs. 0.15 for the S&P 500. A comparison using the monthly Sharpe Ratio yielded similar results (0.22 vs. 0.16, respectively), confirming the relative efficiency of the BXM over the 219-month study period.
- The BXM underperformed the S&P 500 during most rising equity markets and consistently outperformed the S&P 500 in all periods of declining equity markets, demonstrating the return cushion provided by income from writing the calls.
- The BXM generates a return pattern different from that of the S&P 500, offering a source of potential diversification. The addition of the BXM to a diversified investor portfolio would have generated significant improvement in risk-adjusted performance over the past 18 years.

So we can conclude several things about a plain vanilla buy-write. Over the course of time it closely tracks the standard return of the underlying index or stock. It underperforms in rallies and outperforms in declines. "Outperform" of course is of the "less bad" variety. And it exhibits less volatility, enough so that you certainly increase risk-adjusted returns and quite often even absolute returns.

All of this of course makes common sense. The upside of a buy-write? Cushion into a decline, or added income in a slow rally. The downside? You give away your potential to benefit in an extended lift. And you may mistake "income" for "risk," such as in 2008 when buy-writes imploded.

## Want to Trade a Buy-Write?

How do you trade a buy-write? For a normal stock, you have about as easy a leg as you can get; just sell a call against every 100 shares you own.

And replicating this BXM? You can do it yourself quite simply. BXMs hypothetically sell the nearest to the money, near month call. You can just do it for real via futures or ETFs.

You also have several open-end funds dedicated to this, or a similar strategy. And you have a closed-end fund, symbol BEP, that tracks BXM. Of course a closed-end fund has its own issues. Instead of a stream of dividends as if you owned a basket of SPX stocks or the SPY, BEP accumulates them and then disperses semiannually. So you need awareness of the timing of the dispersions.

A bigger consideration however, is that like all closed-end funds, BEP trades at premiums and discounts to net asset value (NAV). Take the stretch from 2006 into April of 2007. The graph in Figure 12.1 compares BEP to its net asset value.

Long story short, BEP traded as much as 20 percent above its NAV. This is extremely odd behavior for a very easy-to-replicate closed-end fund.

And of course, that premium proved illusory. Figure 12.2 shows that same graph covering 2008.

And lo and behold, it actually traded at a deep discount for much of the fall 2008 carnage.

Buying a closed-end ETF at a discount and/or shorting it at a premium always makes sense of course. If you can wait out the inevitable correction. But I digress. We're here to talk about buy-writes.

**Figure 12-1**　BEP vs. NAV, April 2006–April 2007, via StockCharts.com

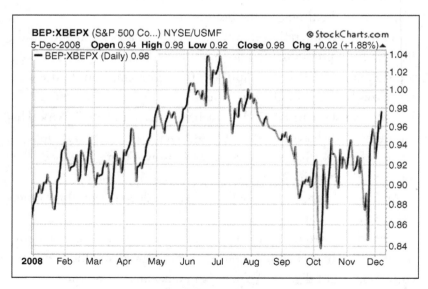

**Figure 12-2**　BEP vs. NAV, 2008, via StockCharts.com

## Strike while the Iron Is Hot?

So how should one go about timing a buy-write?

In Chapter 5 we note that there are certain dates in the expiration cycle that over time prove favorable to options sales. And a buy-write is the definition of an options sale. But this assumes volatility in a vacuum.

Any time volatility spikes, the chattering pundit orchestra takes to the airways and recommends buy-writing.

In all fairness, the chattering pundit orchestra always recommends buy-writing. And for good reason. As all the studies above show, it's a solid strategy, achieving virtually identical returns to the market with reduced risk

But does tweaking the play as volatility moves augment the returns?

In other words, should we get more aggressive, slapping on buy-writes when volatility spikes? Evidence would suggest that, at best, it's a strategy that spins its wheels. And at worst, buy-writing into volatility spikes is a good idea when the market goes lower. In fact you will have achieved "less bad" when, of course, cash was the best option of all.

First, let's get a few things straight. Buy-writing does work better when volatility lifts. Not enormously so, but better. The CBOE gives us data back to June 1988 to play with, so let's say we dig in and rank each day based on the absolute level of the VXO. And let's say we separate it into deciles and examine the average 30-day return going forward for each decile. In other words, how did the BXM do going forward roughly one month based on differing VXO levels? (See Table 12.1.)

The correlation between the VXO level and the one-month return in BXM is 0.1468.

Higher volatility helped, although I would note that instances of relatively extreme VXO are clustered, so this may "double count" results in certain periods. But let's leave that be for now, because we are going to apply that same methodology to the SPX itself. (See Table 12.2.)

**Table 12-1**    BXM 30-Day Return by VXO Level

| VXO Rank | Average 30-Day BXM Return |
|---|---|
| Top 10% | 2.2752% |
| 10%–20% | 0.8868% |
| 20%–30% | 0.6074% |
| 30%–40% | 0.7933% |
| 40%–50% | 0.8338% |
| 50%–60% | 1.2532% |
| 60%–70% | 0.8776% |
| 70%–80% | 0.8474% |
| 80%–90% | 0.8511% |
| Bottom 10% | 0.6340% |

**Table 12-2**    SPX 30-Day Return by VXO Level

| VXO Rank | Average 30-Day SPX Return |
|---|---|
| Top 10% | 2.3698% |
| 10%–20% | 0.1710% |
| 20%–30% | 0.0543% |
| 30%–40% | 0.7365% |
| 40%–50% | 0.9274% |
| 50%–60% | 1.1180% |
| 60%-70% | 0.6942% |
| 70%–80% | 0.8135% |
| 80%–90% | 0.9473% |
| Bottom 10% | 0.6188% |

And lo and behold, we find essentially the same thing—the higher the volatility going forward, the generally better return on the SPX, although again, not as impressive as one might think (and possibly even less than meets the eye).

But the real important question to ask here is whether you get any value added by allocating relatively more money into a buy-write or basic index, depending on volatility. And the answer on the surface looks like a big fat no. Taking all the data from June 1, 1988, to December 31, 2007, we compared the difference of the 30-day return in BXM minus the 30-day return in SPX and correlated the results to absolute levels of the VXO. If in fact a spike in implied volatility connoted a relatively propitious time to slap on some buy-writes, one would expect a positive correlation here.

And, in fact, the correlation was .01, about the same correlation you would have if you decided to buy-write on Wednesdays or on any other day, more or less. In other words, the results are random and unrelated.

But what if we parse the data set a bit and separate the sample into those instances where the SPX was higher 30 days out and those when the SPX was lower?

Here it gets interesting. We found 3,045 days when the SPX was higher 30 days out. We break down the average return by decile of ranked VXO, from highest to lowest. (See Table 12.3.)

In these instances, the correlation between the BXM-SPX return difference we discuss above and the VXO is a small but measurable −.11.

All results were negative (SPX returned more than BXM), which makes sense since we included only those days when the market was higher one month out. But *if* the market rallied, lower volatility setups actually proved relatively better times to buy-write. Kind of counterintuitive.

**Table 12-3**   BXM 30-Day Return Minus SPX 30-day Return by VXO Level,
Market Up

| VXO Rank | Average 30-Day BXM Minus SPX Return (in BP) |
|----------|---------------------------------------------|
| Top 10% | −121 bp |
| 10%–20% | −83 bp |
| 20%–30% | −132 bp |
| 30%–40% | −153 bp |
| 40%–50% | −93 bp |
| 50%–60% | −90 bp |
| 60%–70% | −85 bp |
| 70%–80% | −72 bp |
| 80%–90% | −69 bp |
| Bottom 10% | −56 bp |

The results were even more clear in the 1,868 days in the sample where the market was lower 30 days out. Table 12.4 shows that same decile chart.

The correlation here was a relatively robust .37, meaning that higher volatility did in fact correspond to better returns going forward for the BXM relative to the SPX.

If we look at returns three months out instead, we get similar results—a correlation of .33 (for the record, the correlation was −.05 if the market was higher three months out). But again here's the rub. These are instances when the market went lower. So investing here provided wins of the "less bad" variety. Cash trumped both.

Let's put this another way. If you expect a shaky market, a buy-write certainly works better than a straight buy. And the higher the volatility, the less you lose on that buy-write relative to the market. But then

**Table 12-4** BXM 30-Day Return Minus SPX 30-Day Return by VXO Level, Market Down

| VXO Rank | Average 30-Day BXM Minus SPX Return (in BP) |
|---|---|
| Top 10% | 245 bp |
| 10%–20% | 260 bp |
| 20%–30% | 233 bp |
| 30%–40% | 223 bp |
| 40%–50% | 208 bp |
| 50%–60% | 195 bp |
| 60%–70% | 185 bp |
| 70%–80% | 205 bp |
| 80%–90% | 120 bp |
| Bottom 10% | 114 bp |

it begs the question, Why do something bullish to begin with? Obviously we didn't know that the market would decline.

But if in fact we called a "bull" market correctly in general terms, it behooved us to buy-write when volatility was relatively lower, not higher. And that seems to make no sense.

Yet here's a study that seems to bear that out. As written up in *Barron's Striking Price* on November 28, 2005:

Selling call options against stocks has always been popular with investors looking to monetize their shares' upside potential. But with closed-end funds raising $18 billion over the past 16 months in pursuit of this familiar strategy, more people are seeking an edge when writing covered calls. A Lehman Brothers study, which shows how covered-call sellers might improve their returns, could be of some help here.

Covered-call sellers often look for volatile stocks, since these offer richer premiums. "When volatility is high, some investors are tempted to write more calls," says Lehman derivatives strategist Ryan Renicker. "But projected volatility also is highest when the market is pricing in its worst fears." At these junctures, stocks can turn the corner and rally on the slightest bit of good news — a bummer for covered-call sellers who have agreed to cap their stock gains.

No surprise, then, that strategies featuring covered-call selling—also known as overwriting or buy-writing—tend to outperform stocks in flat or declining markets, but lag when stocks surge. Because returns depend so substantially on the direction of the underlying stocks, "overwriting strategies that are dynamically rebalanced ahead of large market rallies or downturns can naturally enhance the returns generated," say Renicker and Lehman's Devapriya Mallick.

To test their theory, Renicker and Mallick constructed a seemingly counterintuitive portfolio that sells fewer calls when volatility is high, and more when volatility and premiums are low. Specifically, they would write just 0.75 of a call against an index when projected volatility is more than one standard deviation above the average, and increase that to 1.25 calls when projected volatility falls more than one standard deviation below average.

The result? This approach drummed up average annual returns of 7.9% between January 1997 and September 2005 — compared with 6.6% for a basic overwriting portfolio (that systematically sells one-month at-the-money calls against the index), and 5.5% for the S&P 500. Applied to the Nasdaq 100, it produced annual returns that averaged 9.8% over the past nine years—compared with 8.8% for the basic overwriting portfolio and 7.1% for underlying index.

So, strange as it sounds, you want to roll into more call shorts when volatility lags, and fewer when volatility lifts.

The study period did not include 2008 and the exploding VIX. But the behavior of BXM relative to SPX was pretty classic. Figure 12.3 provides a graph comparing the two.

The biggest outperformance of BXM relative to SPY occurred in the May to November stretch. What happened then? Figure 12.4 shows the SPY alone. And Figure 12.5 shows the VIX.

So with a market down by over 40 percent and volatility virtually quadrupling bottom to top in half a year, it behooved one to buy-write as opposed to straight-owning stock. The problem was that hiding under a mattress worked way better than anything.

How about if we tweak it a little more? The CBOE also created an index, symbol BXY, that does essentially the same thing as BXM, except it sells calls approximately 2 percent above the money each

**Figure 12-3**   BXM vs. SPY, 2008, via StockCharts.com

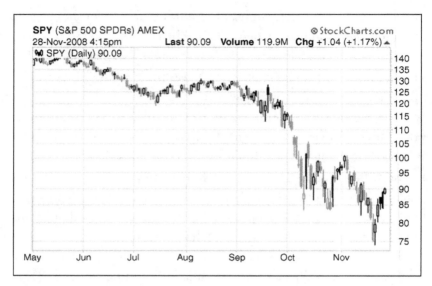

**Figure 12-4**   SPY May–November 2008, via StockCharts.com

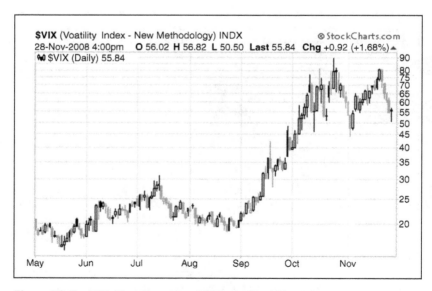

**Figure 12-5**   VIX May–November 2008, via StockCharts.com

month.By applying some similar metrics as the ones we used above, we find the results remarkably similar, with the obvious tweak that BXY acts modestly better in rallies and worse in declines.

And the relationship to volatility virtually duplicates that of BXM. Again, we find the volatility when you slap on a buy-write has virtually a nonexistent correlation to the degree to which BXY out- or underperforms the SPX either one or three months out. But if you separate it into those instances where SPX rallied, absolute VXO level has a –.155 correlation. So in other words, in up markets, you did relatively better with a buy-write if you put it on at a lower volatility. But as with BXM before, you lost less in BXY in down markets, as we found a correlation of .334.

## An Enigma Wrapped Inside a Puzzle . . .

So we are left with a real conundrum. Common sense says that a buy-write becomes more attractive when volatility spikes. But if you translate that into an actual trade, it will work to your benefit only when the market declines in which case you have lost money, just less than you lost via a straight SPX purchase.

How can this possibly make sense? We have to internalize the notion that options volatility does not price in a vacuum. It represents real market expectations for actual volatility. And over the virtually 20 years of data, the net of those expectations in SPX, the busiest of index products, proved pretty accurate.

In fact, you can conclude that outperformance of a buy-write depends on the relationship between implied volatility of the options and realized volatility of the underlying index over the time in question. If you short options as part of a buy-write, or really in any play, you likely cost yourself money one way or another if realized volatility ultimately exceeds implied volatility. Of course we do not know where realized volatility will be when we initiate the buy-write. And the evidence shows that the market ultimately does a good predicting job. Although far from perfect, for as we saw in Chapter 4, volatility does a better job of reflecting what already has happened than it does in predicting the future.

But there must be some inefficiencies somewhere. How can we optimize this thing? What if we go to longer-dated options?

In January 2007, Nikunj Kapadia and Edward Szado evaluated returns for a mechanical buy-write (covered call) strategy based on the Russell 2000 Index. The study period went from January 18, 1996, to November 16, 2006, covering a pretty good cross-section of markets. From the irrational exuberance in 1996 to incredibly irrational exuberance in 1999 to the bear market of 2000–2003 to the quiet and low volatility bull market of February 2003 to late 2006. They used similar methodology to the BXM, but also studied two-month options and concluded the following:

> In contrast to the 1-month strategy, the 2-month at-the-money strategy, in general, underperforms. The underperformance holds for both the entire period as well as the longer of the two sub-periods of January 1996 to February 2003. It is only in the shorter sub-periods of February 2003 to November 2006 that the 2-month at-the-money strategy outperforms the Russell 2000 index. Certainly, at least part of this underperformance is due to the fact that the 2-month implementation adjusts the strikes less frequently so has a greater opportunity for the out-of-the-money call to expire deep in-the-money.

What else is interesting here? That 2003–2006 period corresponded to historically low levels of implied volatility. So it suggests again, counterintuitively, that when volatility lagged, the right play was to commit to shorting it for a longer stretch of time.

## Summary

Buy-writing is an excellent strategy, certainly compared to straight equity ownership, provided of course that you realize that you have dual risk here. On the downside, you have to remember the call sales cushion losses, but generally do not eliminate them. On the upside, calls sales cap profits, which will literally drive you nuts regretting the lost opportunity in a strong bull move.

Common sense says that buy-writing when volatility resides at higher levels makes more sense than when it is lower. At best, timing to volatility is a wash, and at worst, studies show that you are actually better off buy-writing *more* aggressively at times of depressed volatility.

If we break relative returns into two segments of hindsight, one where we know the market rallied and the other where we know the market declined, we find that buy-writing amidst depressed volatility actually worked better than buy-writing amidst elevated volatility in a bull move, relative to just buying and holding the index. On the flip side, buy-writing elevated volatility did outperform by a greater degree when volatility was elevated *if* we find out in hindsight that the market declined over that stretch.

In other words, you lost less in such circumstances, a rather Pyrrhic victory. The real allocation goal should involve something more along the lines of not owning equities at all.

Given of course that we do not know what the market might do, it's very tough to find any value-added way to time switches from buy-writes to and from straight equity ownership, beyond maybe timing the "write" part of the equation to certain times of the expiration cycle, a subject we explore in grim detail in Chapter 4.

# Chapter 13

# STRATEGY
# ROOM

We dedicated all of Chapter 12 to one single options play—the buy-write. That's just one of many. We're not going to get to every last one here, but let's see how many we can cover.

When you establish an options position, you have no obligation to put one on that has an official name, like calendar spread or iron butterfly. I have been doing this work for 21 years and still sometimes need to check a glossary when someone asks me about a certain play by its formal name, as opposed to, say, "I'm long 10 of these and short 20 of these," or something like that. Trade on a floor for 10 minutes and you may get a position that can't be described with one simple phrase.

And trust me. You will not be tested nor will you make a penny based on your ability to memorize the names of each spread. Rather, your job is to manage your positions.

But for the purposes of a book or Web site, we necessarily must deal with plays that have specific names. So let's jump in and take a practical look at some of the plays out there. We'll do our best to build a tool set here and go from the simplest to the most complex.

## Naked Put

The naked put sounds like an incredibly attractive way to own a stock, doesn't it? Suppose it's early February, and Research in Motion (RIMM) is trading for $55. What if I shorted some March 50 puts? I can get about $2.70 for them right now. Heads, I win. RIMM goes higher between now and expiration. Or at least doesn't go that much lower such that my puts expire either worthless or worth less than $2.70 (RIMM closes $47.30 or higher).

Tails, RIMM goes lower than $47.30, and I get assigned the puts I win too, if I am bullish RIMM. I mean buying RIMM at $47.30 sure beats buying RIMM at $55, right?

In a sense, a glass is half-full optimist sort can book either scenario as a win from a certain perspective. But here's the flip side. You can view either scenario as a loss from another perspective. What if I am bullish RIMM but choose the relatively less aggressive path of shorting puts, as opposed to simply buying stock? RIMM goes up to $70. I make that same $2.70 if I got it semi-wrong and RIMM had gone to $50. No, you won't go broke booking profits, but by the same token you will not call every name correctly. No one does. You need to max out wins. Pocketing a mere $2.70 off a $15 move you called correctly far from maxes out the win.

What about the other direction? RIMM goes below $47.30. Well, that's just a loss. Yes, you lost less than if you had bought RIMM, though possibly not less if you simply bought RIMM with a stop.

At the end of the day, though, I do like the naked put strategy. I just feel that the risk-reward picture does not get correctly analyzed. Too often, traders enter a naked put sale with this mindset, "Sure , I'd love to own RIMM at $47.30, so why not sell these puts"? Why not? Because if RIMM gets below there, the last thing you want to do is own it higher. Figure 13.1 is a chart of RIMM from August 2008 to February 2009.

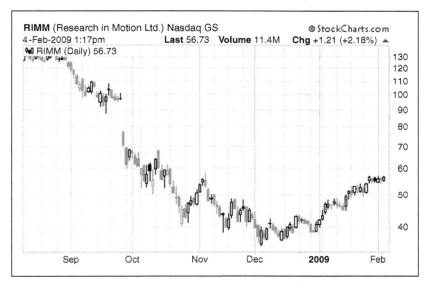

**Figure 13-1**   RIMM, August 2008–February 2009, via StockCharts.com

Along about September, shorting puts with a 100 strike seemed like a great idea. Shorting them with an 80 strike seemed like free money. But RIMM ultimately got as low as 35.

Basically, every stock seems like a steal at prices lower than it is currently trading. This line of thinking would encourage you to short every put.

And another real risk is what we mention above. You love the stock, sell some puts, and make a relative pittance. You won't go broke earning a profit, but you will go broke earning $2.70 and $2.70 there and then getting clunked with some $10 and $20 hits on put sales gone bad.

So here's the mindset I would have when selling puts. You like the stock right here, right now at this price. But you are not afraid of missing too much up side. If that's your feeling, by all means put selling makes good sense. And if this all sounds familiar, like say, it has the same risk-reward picture as a buy-write, I would note that you are 100 percent correct. A buy-write is a synthetic way to create a naked put.

Mind you it's not 100 percent identical. Say RIMM pays a dividend. If you have the buy-write on, you capture that dividend (unless you get assigned the calls you shorted, in which case you will have no position). If you have the naked put on, you do not collect the dividend. In fact, if the dividend was a surprise of some sort, it will actually increase the price of the naked puts at each stock and volatility level.

More on this later, when we discuss dividend capture plays.

## Bull Call Spread

A *bull call spread* is a strategy in which a trader buys a lower strike call and sells a higher strike call to create a trade with limited profit and limited risk. A rise in the price of the underlying increases the value of the spread. Net debit transaction: Maximum loss = debit; Maximum gain = difference between strike prices less the debit, with no margin.

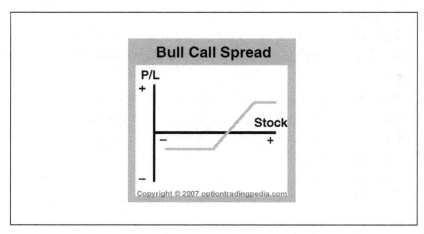

**Figure 13-2**   Bull Call Spread. Graph courtesy of Optionstradingpedia.com

It's a pretty simple play really. Let's say you have a bullish opinion on Apple (AAPL). But you don't have the capital or the risk appetite to buy the stock. You also want defined risk. How about a bull call spread? Say, for example, that AAPL sits at 93, but you think it may hit $100 in the next couple of months. It's January now, so let's buy the March 95-100 call spread for $2.

The risk? That $2 debit. AAPL can go to 80 or 70 or 60, and you still max out at only a $2 loss.

The reward? It's a $5 spread, so you max out at the difference between those $5 and the $2 you paid, for a potential win of $3.

I like bull call spreads in that they have very minimal, often even nonexistent, exposure to moves in volatility. Big, sudden, and often unaccounted for swings in volatility can wreck many an options play. Such a move has very muted impact here though.

Take the AAPL spread above. At the end of January, with about seven weeks to go until expiration, the March 95 calls have a .1405 vega, meaning that for every one-point lift (drop) in volatility, the value of the calls lifts (drops) by 14.05 cents. The March 100 calls have a vega of .1355, so the difference between the two is half a cent. And they will move together. So if AAPL volatility drops by 10 points, the value of the call spread drops by only 5 cents.

But then we have to ask, What are the benefits of buying a call spread here as opposed to simply buying the same dollar amount of calls? In other words, instead of buying 30 call spreads for $2, what if we simply bought 10 March 95 calls at $6, the same exact outlay?

If AAPL closes under $95, both the spread and the calls themselves go worthless, so there's no difference really on a "hold" basis. If AAPL closes between 95 and 100, the call spread did better, perhaps considerably. At $100, for example, the call spread earned $9,000 (three points, 20 times) while the outright call purchase lost $1,000 (one point 10 times). And likewise, the calls have large vega risk. Remember they have a .1405 vega, so an overnight 10-point volatility drop would cost you $1.405 if you straight owned the calls.

Those are the negatives.

On the flip side, straight owning the calls gives you unlimited upside while the call spread maxes out with that $9,000 gain. And you can hedge and trade against a straight-call purchase. Maybe you periodically short stock into strength versus the calls you own and then attempt to buy the stock back cheaper and work off a little bit of the premium you laid out for the calls. It's a position you can actively manage, whereas the bull call spread is almost completely passive. Even though the call spread gets you modestly long, you can't trade stock aggressively against it.

Now perhaps you consider that active management aspect a "bug" and not a feature. You'd rather just make the bet and let it ride. If that's the case, the bull call spread makes the most sense for you. Personally, I trade. It's what I do, I prefer to have a position I can tweak, good or bad. But that's just me.

## Bear Put Spread

A *bear put spread* is a strategy in which a trader sells a lower strike put and buys a higher strike put to create a trade with limited profit and limited risk. A fall in the price of the underlying increases the value of the spread. Net debit transaction: Maximum loss = difference between strike prices less the debit with no margin.

There's not a whole lot of difference between a bear put spread and a bear call spread, short of the obvious one. The bear put spread is a low-risk/low-reward bearish bet. In the above AAPL example, it's buying, say, the March 90–85 put spread.

I would just as soon buy the same dollar amount of puts and take my chances trading against them.

However, note that a bear put spread is not an exact mirror of a bull call spread. Remember, volatility tends to skew such that the lower the strike, the higher the volatility. So when you buy a bull call spread, you probably have paid a modestly higher volatility for the call you own (the March 95s in this case) than the call you sell (the March 100s). Conversely, when you buy a put spread, you probably pay a lower volatility for the put you own than the put you sell.

So you have a small volatility advantage trading the put vertical. But of course, this play is really about your directional bet. And it's important to note that the volatility advantage you may see when you put it on will also be a volatility disadvantage when you take it off. If the product has a "normal" skew, it will likely always have a normal skew.

## Backspreads

A *backspread* is a spread in which more options are purchased than sold and where all options have the same underlying and expiration date. Backspreads are usually delta neutral.

Take this AAPL again. Conversely, a put backspread maybe involves shorting 10 March 95 calls at 6, and buying 20 March 105 calls at $2.50. Or maybe shorting 10 March 90 puts at $5 and buying 20 March 80 puts at $2.25. Something like that. The idea generally is to accumulate extra contracts that eventually translate into positive gamma on a move toward and through the long strike, while at the same time doing the backspread for a credit.

How can you win?

Well, you have two bites of the apple (or AAPL if you prefer). Let's say that we just try the call side. We take in a $1,000 credit putting the spread on (10 x $600) – (20 x $250). We have an opportunity for a small win if AAPL tanks and/or simply expires under $95 in March. Everything goes out worthless.

And we have an opportunity for a big win if AAPL explodes. We have gone long 10 extra calls by virtue of the spread. In this particular example, if we do nothing and just let it go until expiration, you break even at $114, and then ride 10 long calls anywhere above that.

How can you lose?

On an expiration basis, a close right at $105 is the worst case. You lose $4,000 on your short calls and $5,000 on your long calls for a total of $9,000.

The reality of the spread, though, is that you have the position on for a couple months and likely trade against it if AAPL does anything but completely tank. Remember, it gives you a long gamma position to play with. If you know AAPL will go back straight to $200, you sit and do nothing. But of course you do not know that. So you probably start shorting stock into strength over $100 and attempt to flip around against those extra calls.

So basically it's a spread that benefits on an increase in volatility. If that volatility translates into a decline, at least you pocket the net premium. If that translates into an upside move, you have plenty of trading opportunities around your calls.

Worst case is a slow walk higher. Even if it does not close right at $105, the sluggish move will likely draw you into mistakes too early.

Now like the bull and bear spreads earlier in the chapter, you always have a small volatility advantage putting on a call backspread. The calls you buy almost always trade "cheaper" in volatility terms than the calls you sell. Conversely, a put backspread will find you buying relatively fat puts.

Despite that, I actually prefer putting on put backspreads, depending on the specifics to each trade of course. Volatility tends to get explosive in sell-offs, so that extra little bit you pay initially tends to come back to you in spades if the stock tanks. In fact that is almost precisely why I like this play. Stocks generally lift slowly, so when this happens, you earn the small net premium you take in. Likewise they tend to drop on relatively higher volatility, which gives you a little kicker in addition to your long gamma.

I also like this trade as a combo, Put backspread versus call backspread. We know only one side max will be in a play at a give time; we just don't know which one. But if we do both sides, we earn that small premium from the side that's not in play.

In this example, suppose we do both sides. AAPL goes higher. I have the long gamma at around the 105 level and an extra $500 eventually thanks to the put backspread. Likewise if AAPL tanks, I have that extra $1,000 from the ultimately worthless call premium.

Again though, the toughest case is a slow drift to a long strike, which in practice happens more in a rally than in a decline.

## Calendar Call Spread

A *calendar call spread* is a spread consisting of one long and one short option of the same type with the same exercise price, but which expire in different months.

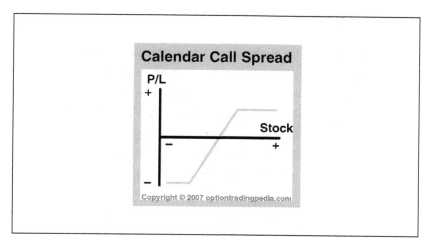

**Figure 13-3**  Calendar Call Spread. Graph courtesy of Optionstradingpedia.com

How about we stick with the AAPL theme? We'll look at a three-month calendar. Say now it's March expiration, so we'll buy the July 95 calls and short the April 95s. For ease of explanation (and graphing) the Aprils have 30 days until expiration, while the Julys have 120 days.

If you own a calendar and sit with it until expiration, you max out if the stock closes as near to strike price as possible. The calls you shorted go to zero or near zero. The calls you own go to, well, we don't know exactly. It depends on where July volatility trades on April expiration day.

A calendar spread is the sort of spread you can sit and do nothing with—just let nature take it's course. The spread gives you negative gamma as the calls you shorted have a higher gamma than the calls you own as well as positive time decay as the shorter option drips value faster. In this case, assuming we have bought and sold identical volatility of 45. The Aprils have a gamma of .0331, meaning that for each one-point lift (decline) in AAPL, the delta of the April 95 calls lifts (declines) by .0331. And the Julys have a .0166 gamma, for a net gamma of −0.132. So you do get modestly longer into weakness and shorter into strength. But you have very limited risk and reward since you can lose only the net debit you paid and earn only some realistic max out in a well-timed volatility lift.

I look at calendar spreads as two-pronged volatility plays. One half of the play is a near-month volatility short. You tend to win or lose on a simple near-month options sale based on how the implied volatility you sold compares to the realized volatility in the stock between the time of the trade and expiration. Longer-term options volatility trends have relatively muted impact on a short-dated option.

The other half of the play, the 120-day options you own? Well, the nearer an option to expiration, the more that current HV dictates pricing. The further out in time, the more "mean reversion" assumptions come into play, and the less current volatility tweaks matter. So 90-day to 120-day is kind of at the crossroads of the two; somewhat sensitive to nearer-term stock volatility and somewhat sensitive to longer-term mean reversion.

Despite the attraction of earning positive decay with muted risk, I tend to shy away from calendar spreads. There are too many moving parts, and it's not as easy as it seems to guess where a stock may trade a month from now. I would have to really like the volatility setup and have a strong conviction that the stock will move little over the next month while, at the same time, consider that longer-term options are priced attractively enough to want to own them. But keep in mind that this very inactivity over the next month that we are rooting for will necessarily weigh on longer-term options. A month of dull trading will simply cause buyers to lower those mean reversion estimates we noted.

It's also important to mention that a specific volatility spread between the two cycles in and of itself does not make a calendar spread attractive. What if, instead of AAPL, we look at calendars in ABC Biotech and we see that April trades at a 90 volatility, while July sits at a mere 60? And 60 is cheap relative to longer-term volatility trends. Seems like a steal, right?

Well, it's a small biotech. What if some sort of FDA announcement regarding Phase II testing of ABC's one and only product is due out some time between now and April expiration? And since it's a small biotech, ABC will likely make a huge move on the news. It's entirely possible that owning 90 volatility in the near month and shorting 60 volatility in the outer month makes the most sense of all.

## Backspread and Calendar Spread Combined

You can combine a backspread and calendar spread. Maybe you buy outermonth calls and/or puts with strikes away and out of the money and short a smaller number of nearer-month and nearer money calls.

You're not going to do this for a credit to you unless you go *way* wide on the options you own.

I don't really love this play, but I do like it better as a way to accumulate some longer-dated gamma, particularly if you combine a put play with a call play.

Say in this AAPL we buy 20 July 115 calls for $2.80 each and 20 July 65 puts for $1 versus shorting 10 April 100 calls for $2.25 and 10 April 80 puts for 0.75. If AAPL closes somewhere between 80 and 100 on April expiration, we have accumulated 20 strangles at a price that will likely prove attractive, pending how much July volatility has contracted. Just don't forget that July options have withstood a month of decay themselves.

Should AAPL move one direction before the Aprils expire, we have extra calls (or puts). But of course we likely have a small loser on the side that is out of play now, say the puts if AAPL is trading 125.

All in all, I like this better than a straight calendar spread in that it at least has the potential to become tradable. But I'd sooner just keep it simple, let someone else game the volatility curve, and just do a backspread.

## Butterfly Spread

The *butterfly spread* is a neutral options trading strategy that is a combination of a bull spread and a bear spread. It is a limited-profit, limited-risk options strategy. There are three strike prices involved in a butterfly spread, and it can be constructed using calls or puts.

So I'm looking at, hey, AAPL. It's January again, and I have interest in buying a March call butterfly. So I buy 10 March 95 calls for $5.50, short 20 March 100 calls for $3.50, and buy 10 March 105 calls for $2. So that's a net debit of 50 cents.

What am I gaming?

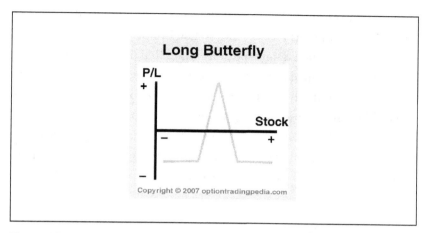

**Figure 13-4**   Long Butterfly. Graph courtesy of Optionstradingpedia.com

It's essentially a neutral play from every angle. No serious volatility exposure, not much delta exposure until it gets very near expiration, and not much time decay, again, until the very end.

So why bother?

Good question.

If you buy a butterfly, you always pay a debit. That is your risk. If AAPL closes anywhere under 95 or over 105 on March expiration, you lose the 50 cents you paid. That's the risk side of the equation.

The reward side is that the maximum value of the butterfly, which will always happen at the middle strike and which will always be $5 minus the debit you pay. So, in this case, you earn $4.50. Every penny off $100 is subtracted from $4.50 down to (up to) $95.50 ($104.50), at which point you break even.

So it's a low-risk/low-reward bet that AAPL closes near $100.

I personally would not bother with straight butterflies. They're like shooting fish in a barrel. But they sound attractive. I mean let's say if you are bullish on AAPL, why not try this? You just need a modest rally over two months, and you will make some money. But the reality is that no one has all that much insight into where a stock might close on one isolated date, especially when that date is a month or two away. To me, it's just a way to say you are playing, while not risking much — or potentially gaining much. And to get it on at decent prices, it will likely require some legging, executing one side of a multi-part trade and gambling you will do the balance at a favorable price to you, which is fine and will likely cost little in an active and tight option like AAPL, but it's not so simple for a smaller-name stock.

## Iron Butterfly

The *iron butterfly* is the combination of a long (short) straddle and a short (long) strangle. All options must have the same underlying and have the same expiration.

Translating to our AAPL, the iron butterfly would involve buying the AAPL March 95 straddle and shorting the March 85 puts and March 105 calls.

For argument's sake, let's say we pay a total of $7 for the package. It's quite simple to analyze an iron butterfly. You risk the total debit, in this case $7, if the stock closes at the strike where you own the straddle. You max out if it goes to or exceeds either side of the strangle. You can earn up to the wider strike difference of the call or put side, less the premium you pay. Both are 10 points in this example, so you will earn $3 if AAPL closes below 85 or above 105.

There's not all that much to distinguish between a regular butterfly and an iron butterfly, except, of course, that an iron butterfly uses both calls and puts. But the principle for both is the same. You are essentially picking a strike and betting either it closes close to it (if you buy a regular butterfly or short an iron butterfly) or far from it (if you short a regular butterfly or purchase an iron butterfly).

I feel the same way about these as I do about regulars. I don't find they accomplish all that much. And they have the added twist of your needing to leg an extra series.

## Condors

A *condor* is a four-series trade involving the sale (purchase) of the lowest and highest strike and a purchase (sale) of two middles strikes. The same class, expiration, and quantity apply in all four series.

There's not much difference between a basic condor and a basic butterfly. With the condor, you add another strike in the middle, but it's really the same sort of bet. If I'm buying the wings, I am going to pay a modest debit for the condor. If the condor closes below the lowest strike or above the highest strike, I lose that premium. My maximum win is a close at either of the middles strikes I sold or any point in between.

A condor will really make sense over a butterfly in a name with many strikes that are in play—like an ETF, say SPY, with $1 strikes,

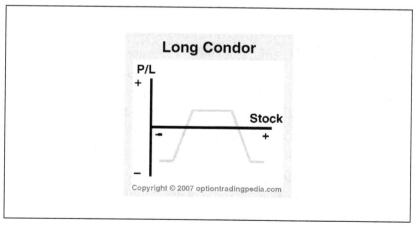

**Figure 13-5**  Long Condor. Graph courtesy of Optionstradingpedia.com

or maybe a high dollar value stock like GOOG. Generally speaking though, it always pays to keep it simple. There's no particular edge to a condor over a butterfly, so generally better to stick to as few strikes and series as possible.

## Iron Condor

An *iron condor* is a sale (purchase) of an OTM call spread combined with a sale (purchase) of an OTM put spread. The same class, expiration, and quantity apply in all four series.

This is a strategy we can nail down. Its got a great name, and it's strategy I actually like.

An iron condor provides a pure limited-risk/limited-reward bet against volatility.

Back to AAPL again, with the stock at 93. We will sell 10 March 85–90 put spreads for $1.70 and sell 10 March 100–105 call spreads for $1.50. Should AAPL expire in March between 90 and 100, we pocket that entire combined premium of $3.20. Should AAPL close below 85 or above 105, we lose $5, minus the premium we took in, or $1.80. We break even at $86.80 and $103.20, and then lose $10 each penny down from $86.80 to 85 and from $103.20 to 105.

There's very little options volatility exposure here. All four series will move pretty much in lockstep. If you have large skew, it would balance out also as you will own both the fattest volatility series of the trade (the 85 puts) and the cheapest (the 105 calls). You also have no reason to get shaken out one way or another. If you have this on, you are capped every which way.

All in all, it's a solid play. Butterflies require that you get kind of precise with your price target. Iron condors require a more general bet on both the range and overall volatility.

## Synthetics

There's a bunch of these:

- *Synthetic short put:* A short call and a long stock or future.
- *Synthetic long call:* A long put and a long stock or future.
- *Synthetic long put:* A long call and a short stock or future.
- *Synthetic long stock:* A short put and a long call.
- *Synthetic short call:* A short put and a short stock or future.
- *Synthetic short put:* A short call and a long stock or future.

A synthetic is basically just a more complicated way to enter a simple trade. So why do it?

Let's take the example of a synthetic put. Often calls trade tighter and deeper than corresponding puts, particularly when the call sits just out of the money. The put may even have a modest premium over parity with the call. Perhaps there's thought that the underlying company will raise its dividend. Maybe the stock has gotten difficult to borrow. These are both common events and have the net effect of causing puts to trade modestly fat.

So let's say you want to buy some puts but don't want to pay that extra premium. Then you are better off buying the call of the same strike and expiration and shorting the stock.

When I traded on the AMEX, before the elimination of the plus-tick rule and before instantaneous automation and before decimals and before dual listings, pretty much all calls traded "cheaper" than their corresponding puts. You had to exercise real caution selling puts in any kind of size because you often could go quite some time before getting a stock short off to hedge the trade. Plus the order flow was almost all of the sell-call or buy-put variety. So we always quoted calls cheap and puts high. If I wanted to buy a put, it was way more economical to buy it the synthetic way.

Now it's many years and many developments later, and there's really no disparity any more without a good reason (like difficulty or inability to borrow). I am still conditioned to look for cheap calls if I want to actually leg into a put trade, but there's no real reason to do that any more. Everything is in line.

## Collars

Suppose you own AAPL. Just plain old AAPL, the stock. And you have had a nice ride in AAPL. You want to give it more room to run, but you'd like to lock in some profit too.

How about a collar?

What is a *collar*? It's a combo trade where you simultaneously short OTM calls and purchase OTM puts, typically for close to even money.

In AAPL, with the stock near 95, it could mean selling March 100 calls versus buying March 90 puts. For argument's sake, we'll say we own 1,000 shares, and we want to "flatten," so we enter the collar 10 times.

The net effect of this trade is that you now have a position on that is for all intents and purposes equal to the bull call spread we discuss earlier in the chapter. The 10 March 90 puts versus the 1,000 shares of stock you own is a synthetic long position of 10 March 90 calls. So you essentially now own the March 90–100 bull call spread.

Why is this attractive? Taken from the original motivation of the trade, it makes perfect sense. You have presumably scored a win on AAPL. You now effectively stop yourself out at 90, while you're still participating in a ride up to 100. If you initiate the whole package at once though, it's just a bull call spread with an extra leg.

## Stock Repair

Stock repair is not an official strategy. Much like a collar provides a play around a winning position, stock repair seeks to fix a sunken stock in your portfolio. And to me, it's a play that makes less sense than taking a cell phone call while walking next to Jessica Alba.

So what is stock repair? Here's a piece on it from the October 15, 2008, edition of *Barron's*:

> Most repair strategies are based on buying a one-by-two ratio call spread for several months, creating two positions: 1) a covered write and 2) a long bull spread. In many instances, you should be able to initiate the strategy for even-money or even a small credit.
>
> Since we are selling twice as many calls as we are buying, the value of premiums collected should offset the cost of the option being purchased. If that does not work out, look into moving strikes and/or changing expiration months.
>
> We would not necessarily forsake the idea if there were a small debit. The goal is for the stock to rise above the upper strike price. If that does occur, the shares from the covered write would be called away, likely for a loss. The remaining bull spread should be closed for, theoretically, the difference between the two exercise prices. The latter is expected to offset the loss from the former. Any credits or dividends received would be added to the net result.
>
> The main objective in creating the strategy is to lower the break-even point. An added benefit occurs if a profit potential arises. That should not be the target, however, the goal is to break even.

A little confusing play, but the writer adds an example to help illustrate:

The best way to illustrate the strategy is to look at an example. A stock was purchased at $72.20 and is currently trading at $52.71, down 27%. For each 100 shares of stock, we purchase one 3-month call with a 52-$^1/_2$ strike and sell two calls with a 62-$^1/_2$ strike for a $0.50 net credit.

The covered write is long 100 shares and short 1 call with a 62-1/2 strike. The vertical call spread is long one option with a 52-1/2 strike and short 1 option with a 62-1/2 strike. If the shares rise above the $62.50 level, the shares will likely be sold for a loss of $9.70 per share. The theoretical value of the spread is $10 per share, creating a profit of $0.30 per share. Add in the credit of $0.50 and we have a profit of $0.80 per share—without putting additional capital at risk. We note that the trade must be maintained in a margin account.

As the author notes, if the stock goes lower, there's no incremental gain from this strategy.

And therein lies the problem with the play, in my humble opinion. What do you actually accomplish?

I don't find stock repair necessarily a bad idea, but to me it's two separate things: the original losing stock position, with which stock repair has done nothing to hedge, and the new 2:1 call spread you just put on. A ratio spread call spread in a broken stock sounds fine as a stand-alone position. If such a stock lifts, the volatility probably caves in, and the calls you sold will underperform.

What would I do instead of stock repair? The best suggestion is always to just take the loss and move on to the next trade. Last time I checked, we had no laws against reentering a long at a higher price with a better backdrop.

But let's say you want to maintain your upside exposure for whatever reason. To me, I'd sooner do something almost diametrically opposite and buy a put backspread. Suppose you own 100 shares of stock. What if you buy four OTM puts against it and simultaneously short two ATM puts? For argument's sake, we will do it for even, or a small credit.

This play actually does address the stock position; it effectively stops it out at some level. You have now in fact gotten yourself long one extra put per 100 shares of your original position.

On the flip side, if the stock rallies back, it's no harm no foul. You have possibly taken in a small credit.

## Dividend Plays

Dividend plays can take many forms, but when they refer to options, they generally involve two players crossing a spread between two deep in-the-money calls for the intrinsic value of the spread. This generally takes place on the day before a stock trades ex-dividend.

For example, let's say we have hypothetical stock XYZ trading for $85 about a week ahead of February expiration. Tomorrow, XYZ pays a 50-cent dividend.

XYZ stock has strikes every five points down to $50. And some of those lower strikes have decent open interest in the calls. Trader A might say to Trader B, "Hey, why don't we put on the Feb. 65–70 call spread?" Trader B looks and sees that the Feb. 65 calls have an open interest of 3,000 and the Feb. 70s have an open interest of 4,000.

So Trader B says, "Sure, let's put it up."

And what they do is cross the spread on some exchange for $5, we'll say 1,000 times. We'll also say Trader A bought the spread, getting her long the 65 calls.

So what's going on here?

Trader A and Trader B each want to capture that 50-cent dividend. How can they do that? By shorting a call that's deep enough in the money that the value of the dividend is greater than the value of the corresponding put and then not getting assigned the call ahead of when the stock trades ex-dividend. But you can't just short the call and cross your fingers. That's akin to simply shorting the stock.

Thus what generally goes on is a spread such as the one above. Two traders cross a spread between two deep calls. Each then immediately exercises the calls he or she just bought.

The attraction, the magnet so to speak, is open interest. You want to short the series with the most open interest and least risk possible. That's your only chance to "get away" with some dividends; hope someone who already owns the calls does not remember to exercise them for the dividend. By "least risk" I mean deepest in the money. If you do a dividend spread and get away with some, you have a de facto naked put short on the line of calls you sold. In the above spread, if Trader A does not get assigned all the Feb. 70 calls she sold, she now has a buy-write on the Feb. 70 line (remember, she exercised all the Feb. 65 calls she bought).

In this example, it's probably not enormous risk. We said the stock was $85, so she's effectively now short Feb. 70 puts with a week to go. And it's important to note, she can completely lock in the trade by purchasing as many Feb. 70 puts as she is now short calls. And as long as she purchases them for under 50 cents, she has locked in the difference between 50 cents and the price of the puts. With an asterisk.

Okay, the asterisk (*) is that she makes a little less. She has transaction cost on the big spread and possibly an exercise and/or assignment charge. And she has to carry the long stock versus the short call and long put position for a week. The carry for a week of course is not much in any interest rate environment, much less the one that existed in early 2009.

The transaction cost is important though with respect to dividend spreads. Different players have different arrangements when they put these on. No one will do them without a favorable cost treatment because it's a lottery ticket sort of play. Most calls that should get exercised for a dividend do get exercised for the dividend. You may need to try this 50 or 100 times before you get lucky. Because keep in mind that Trader A and Trader B are far from the only two people who try this. An open interest of 3,000 in the above example might generate 10,000 or 20,000 or 30,000 or even more spreads going up trying to capture it. All often for naught.

Basically, it's unlikely anyone but a floor trader/market maker sort or a large desk even tries these, but they're worth highlighting just to note a common trade.

## Summary

I have thrown out a handful of defined strategies and my opinions on them. If I had to pick a couple here I like, I would pick variations of the naked put sale, the backspread, and the iron condor plays.

Collars are fine as a way to lock in a little something after a favorable move in a position. The ugly cousin of "stock repair"? Not so much in my humble opinion. I would prefer protecting a loser position with a trade that actually stops out that loser at some level.

But I can't emphasize strongly enough that we have no rules that state that an options position has to fall into one of these specific plays. You can set it up any way you see fit. The considerations are always your capital requirements and your risk/reward parameters.

# Chapter 14

# ULTRA AND
# INVERSE ETFs

There is more to options and volatility trading than simply trading options and direct volatility products.

In 2007, ProShares introduced a series of leveraged ETFs that resemble a bit of a hybrid of every derivative known—part option, part index, part ETF.

Is this the breakaway star? Clearly SKF in early to mid-2008. What does SKF do? This, from ProShares:

> UltraShort Financials ProShares seeks daily investment results, before fees and expenses, that correspond to twice (200%) the inverse (opposite) of the daily performance of the Dow Jones U.S. Financials Index SM.

In December 2007, volume in SKF, the ultra inverse bank shares, averaged 2.7 million shares per day. By June 2008, that number had hit 15.7 million per day. In October 2008, it went north of 28 million. And it became the de facto tail wagging the dog. Before inverses and ultras, XLF represented the most popular vehicle to make a comprehensive bet on the financial sector. I calculated an approximate dollar volume of both XLF and SKF (volume × closing share price for XLF, 2 × volume × share price in SKF since it represents a 200 percent move) and then added them up and looked at SKF's share of that total volume for each month. The results are shown in Table 14.1.

So SKF has grown from not even a 1 percent share of the financial ETF "bet" in May 2007 to over 60 percent by the middle of 2008. And the product listed only at the end of January 2007.

The story is similar for the options. Figure 14.1 show options volume from November 2007 to November 2008.

Figure 14.2 shows open interest for the same time period.

**Table 14-1**  SKF Dollar Volume (Adusted) as % of Combined SKF/XLF Volume

| Date | Dollar-Adjusted SKF Volume as a Percent of Combined SKF and XLF Volume |
|---|---|
| May 2007 | .55% |
| June 2007 | 1.34% |
| July 2007 | 3.27% |
| August 2007 | 5.44% |
| September 2007 | 5.60% |
| October 2007 | 6.59% |
| November 2007 | 13.36% |
| December 2007 | 18.18% |
| January 2008 | 20.21% |
| February 2008 | 30.73 |
| March 2008 | 42.60% |
| April 2008 | 45.34% |
| May 2008 | 46.93% |
| June 2008 | 55.63% |
| July 2008 | 66.90% |
| August 2008 | 71.42% |
| September 2008 | 61.31% |
| October 2008 | 65.78% |

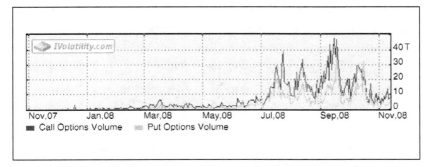

**Figure 14-1**   SKF Options Volume, November 2007–November 2008
via iVolatility.com

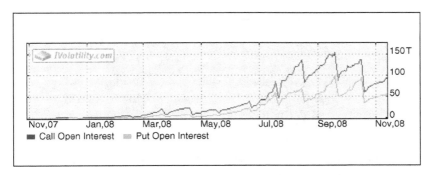

**Figure 14-2**   SKF Open Interest, November 2007–November 2008
via iVolatility.com

It essentially went from a random order here and there to a product that traded over 40,000 calls and 30,000 puts some days in October 2008. And cumulative open interest got up to nearly 250,000 contracts.

How monstrous is this? Let's go back to the structure of SKF itself. It tracks 200 percent of the daily inverse move in the IShares Dow Jones US Financial Index IYF. At the time of peak volume, SKF carried a price tag of 150 or so compared to a price tag in the 50s for IYF, the underlying ETF. When you factor in the price ratio between the two and that each SKF contract gives you 200 percent of the move in IYF, you have to multiply that volume and open interest by almost six to quantify the bets on the underlying.

Again though, IYF never served as the best ETF proxy for the banking sector. That title would go to XLF, an almost identical mover, but an S&P product. It's a "select SPYder" that tracks all the financial stocks in the S&P 500.

Figure 14.3 shows XLF options volume over the same time frame as above. And Figure 14.4 shows open interest.

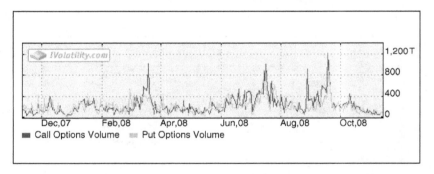

**Figure 14-3**  SKF Options Open Interest, November 2007–November 2008, via iVolatility.com

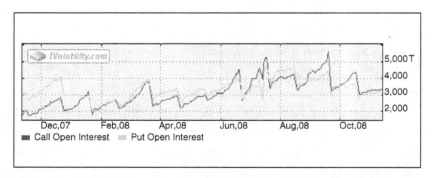

**Figure 14-4**  XLF Options Open interest November 2007-November 2008 courtesy of iVolatility.com

Keep in mind that XLF averaged a price of roughly $20 in September and October 2008, so one contract in SKF equaled about 15 contracts in XLF at the time.

So multiply the volumes accordingly, and you can see that SKF options went from essentially a zero share of the pie in November 2007 to numbers varying from 30 to 50 percent of the total dollar-adjusted options share by September and October 2008.

But wait, there's more. Figure 14.5 shows a graph of the 30-day normalized volatility of SKF options from November 2007 to November 2008.

So most of that volume went up on or around peak options pricing in volatility terms.

Yes, the tail of the inverse was starting to wag the financial dog in options as well as the stocks themselves. And it wasn't just the banks. Double inverse such as SDS (S&P Index), QID (Nasdaq 100) and DUG (IYE) took flight.

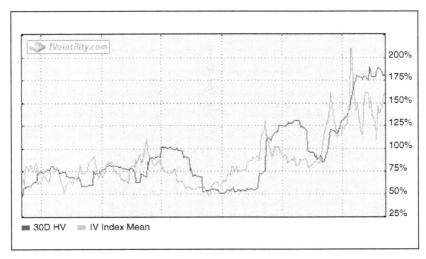

**Figure 14-5**   SKF 30 Day Implied Volatility November 2007–November 2008 via Ivolatility.com

As it turned out, doubles became kind of the "gateway leveraged ETF." In November 2008, Direxion listed a family of triples.

The following is from *Morningstar* on November 5, 2008.

> Market-timers rejoice! Today, Boston-based Direxion officially launched the first group of exchange-traded funds that offer triple leverage, or 300% exposure to market indexes to make bullish or bearish bets. With excessive financial leverage at the heart of the current credit crises, the timing of this launch may surprise some. Over the past several months market participants have experienced unprecedented levels of volatility. With a dynamic regulatory environment, blitzes of weak economic data, credit markets that have yet to fully thaw, and uncertainty surrounding the new administration, it seems as though volatility may remain for some time. For investors looking to magnify market returns with these aggressive products, we can offer some simple advice: Hold on to your hats.

Ten days later, the Direxion small cap bull 3x shares (TNA), designed to capture 300 percent of the daily move in the Russell 2000, were trading nearly 2 million shares per day. And the Direxion small cap bear 3x shares (TZA) saw 1 million shares.

And these were the mediocre ones. FAZ, which tracks –3x the move in the Russell Financial Index (whatever that is, I have honestly never seen anyone measure financials by this) was trading 3 million shares per day by mid-December. By mid-February that number grew to 16 million per day. Clearly much of that popularity came at the expense of SKF, which saw its exponential growth stall a bit.

So these inverse shares got popular primarily because the market got rather unpopular in 2008, which leads to a few questions for options players. Do they make any sense for the typical trader to play? And if yes, how so? And does their mere presence and popularity perturb options-related sentiment indicators, like the put/call and the VIX?

## So Let's Take a Look under the Hood

Inverse double shares do not track –200 percent of the move over an indefinite amount of time. It's –200 percent of the 1 one-day move. In other words, let's say you want to make a leveraged bet against the Dow Jones Real Estate Index ETF, symbol IYR. ProShares has SRS, designed to return to you 200 percent of the inverse move of IYR. Now let's say IYR declines by 10 percent in the next month. SRS should rally by 20 percent. Right?

Well, not exactly.

ProShares' funds track one-day moves. In fact it describes itself on its Web site this way:

> ProShares are designed to provide either 200%, –200% or –100% of index performance on a *daily basis*(before fees and expenses).
>
> A common misconception is that ProShares should also provide 200%, –200% or –100% of index performance over longer periods, such as a week, month or year. However, ProShares' returns may be greater than—or less than—what you'd expect over longer periods.

Now technically, the company speaks the truth. But ProShares' returns will exceed expected returns over the long term only in one circumstance; an extended directional move that has only the slightest of retracement along the way. Let's look at the Dow Jones U.S. Oil/Gas Index. It began 2008 at $66.50 and ended it at $38.47, down a cool 42.15 percent. (See Figure 14.6.)

And here's DIG. The ProShares' fund was designed to double the returns of IEO. (See Figure 14.7.)

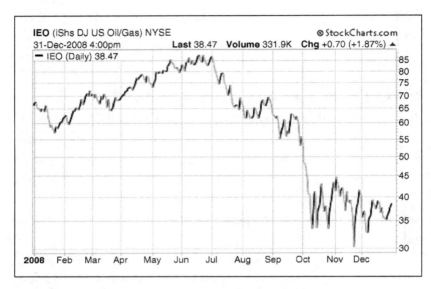

**Figure 14-6**   Dow Jones Oil/Gas Index, 2008 via StockCharts.com

**Figure 14-7**   DIG (ProShares Ultra Oil and Gas), 2008 via StockCharts.com

This is pretty close tracking, Adjust for a $4.29630 distribution in March, and DIG lost 69.72 percent. Outperformance, although the kind we want to do without.

Then we have DUG, designed to track –200 percent of the move in IEO. (See Figure 14.8.)

DUG closed at $35.98 at the end of 2007 and then finished 2008 at $25.04. However, DUG paid out $8.198 in dividends and distributions. So factoring this in, DUG lost only 7.62 percent in 2008.

**Figure 14-8**   DUG (ProShares UltraShort Oil and Gas), 2008 via StockCharts.com

## Hey, What's Going On Here?

With IEO down by over 42 percent, shouldn't DUG be up something at least close to 84 percent, basically DIG in reverse? Is this so poorly managed that it can't keep up?

That's not likely based on either interpretation of the methodology or a viewing of the actual tracking data. ProShares does no better or worse on average than any other typical tracking ETF.

ProShares creates the ETFs by engaging in swaps that are designed to give the ETF the performance it seeks. So in other words, to create a share of DUG, ProShares will buy a custom product from a third party, who will in turn absorb the risk of under- or overperformance.

This is simple compounding math. The underperformance of DUG in 2008 is not a bug. Rather it's a feature of the calculation methodology. Not a promoted feature, mind you, but not a malfunction either.

And it's not just DUG; it's the entire universe of ultras and ultra shorts.

As ProShares notes, these ultras and inverses are the "50 first dates" of ETF products. They have no memory of the day before. They simply come in fresh where they went out the day before and move with the designed relationship to the one-day move of the underlying index. This leads to a simple problem for stockholders the longer they hold onto the shares — compounding.

How does this work in semi-real life? Consider the DIG/DUG/IEO combo, and let's say we start them all at 100 on Day 1. What if IEO goes up by 2 percent per day, for a week? Table 14.2 shows the close each day.

**Table 14.2** Hypothetical Week of IEO/DIG/DUG Trading

|  | IEO | DIG | DUG |
| --- | --- | --- | --- |
| Day 1 | 102 | 104 | 96 |
| Day 2 | 104.04 | 108.16 | 92.16 |
| Day 3 | 106.1208 | 112.4864 | 88.4736 |
| Day 4 | 108.243216 | 116.984856 | 84.932656 |
| Day 5 | 110.40808 | 121.66425 | 81.5353498 |

IEO will close at 110.41, for a rally of 10.41 percent. DIG doubles the daily move up, so it will close at 121.66, a return of 21.66 percent that is notably more than double the IEO gain. Conversely, DUG drifts to 81.54, a drop of 18.46 percent. Increase the run to 10 or 20 or 50 days, change the magnitudes, and so on, and the results are similar.

It sounds great, right? I mean the double inverse loses less than one might expect, and the ultra makes more than double the IEO. What could go wrong?

How about the fact that even in large and persistent trend moves like those we saw in 2008, stocks don't go one direction forever. And any time the underlying revisits any price it visited before, both the ultra and the ultra inverse are worth less than they were the last time they were at that price.

Going back to the above example, how about on Day 6 and Day 7, IEO loses a smidge over $2.70 each and closes at 105 at the end of Day 7. It's a 5 percent gain over the course of seven trading days, but a retracement of barely over one-half of the net gain. Let's add it onto the above table (see Table 14.3).

**Table 14.3** Hypothetical 7 Day IEO/DIG/DUG Trade

|  | IEO | DIG | DUG |
|---|---|---|---|
| Day 1, up 2% | 102 | 104 | 96 |
| Day 2, up 2% | 104.04 | 108.16 | 92.16 |
| Day 3, up 2% | 106.1208 | 112.4864 | 88.4736 |
| Day 4, up 2% | 108.243216 | 116.984856 | 84.932656 |
| Day 5, up 2% | 110.40808 | 121.66425 | 81.5353498 |
| Day 6, down 2.45% | 107.70404 | 115.704813 | 85.5291671 |
| Day 7, down 2.51% | 105 | 109.894995 | 89.8237931 |

DIG would close at 109.89, slightly less than double the gain on IEO, while DUG would close at 89.82, slightly above the "anticipated" 10 percent loss.

Now how about we take IEO back to where it all began at 100. We'll do it over the next two days ($2.50 each day). The results are shown in Table 14.4.

DIG closes at 99.56, while DUG closes at 98.69.

Getting back to the description by ProShares above, ultras and inverses *could* outperform in longer time frames, but only if the underlying ETF or index moves in one direction for an extended stretch. Any sort of pullback or retracement of a move, even a partial one, will lead to underperformance relatively quickly. In the example above, giving back half the move caused both sides to underperform by a small amount, while a full round trip in two weeks begat a .44 percent underperformance on one side, and a whopping 1.31 percent shortfall on the other.

And when you keep in mind that it will happen again and again, you'll see that ownership here for any extended length of time poses

**Table 14.4** Hypothetical IEO/DIG/DUG Trade

|  | IEO | DIG | DUG |
|---|---|---|---|
| Day 1, up 2% | 102 | 104 | 96 |
| Day 2, up 2% | 104.04 | 108.16 | 92.16 |
| Day 3, up 2% | 106.1208 | 112.4864 | 88.4736 |
| Day 4, up 2% | 108.243216 | 116.984856 | 84.932656 |
| Day 5, up 2% | 110.40808 | 121.66425 | 81.5353498 |
| Day 6, down 2.45% | 107.70404 | 115.704813 | 85.5291671 |
| Day 7, down 2.51% | 105 | 109.894995 | 89.8237931 |
| Day 8, down 2.38% | 102.5 | 104.6619 | 94.1011166 |
| Day 9, down 2.44% | 100 | 99.5564415 | 98.691415 |

extreme risks. Wait long enough, and all these products will head to a shoe size. And infact by Summer 2009, FAS and FAZ had declined to shoe sizes, prompting Direxion to reverse split FAS 1:5 and FAS 1:10.

## Fear Not. We Can Tie This All to Volatility

There's something else important to note. Volatility plays a role in how fast it all gets to wallpaper.

What if we essentially halve the daily moves in IEO from the above example? After the nine-day move that gets IEO back where it started, DIG would be worth 99.88, while DUG would trade for 99.66. A mere .12 percent and .34 percent underperformance, although "mere" is only relative to the more volatile first example. Consider that over the course of time, you compound that .12 percent and .34 percent nonerror "error." Before you know it, you have a situation like the real DUG in 2008 that actually declined in a year that saw energy stocks implode.

We can play all sorts of math games here, or we can just summarize with some general rules.

Let's separate the underlying index/ETF into two types of intermediate-term behavior. One is a relatively tight range, say it chops within a 5–10 percent range. If that happens, the above dynamic will play out in spades. Both the inverse and the ultra will drift such that the longer the underlying churns, the more and more each side disappoints.

The other is a trend move in the underlying. Even the best and worst markets give back some gains and recapture parts of losses, so assuming that this is the case, we can fully expect the "winning" side of the ProShares products (i.e., the inverse of a losing ETF, or the ultra of a winner) will way undershoot the "expected" gain, much like the DUG performance above. On the flip side, the losing side, like DIG, will eventually get to a point where compounding works in its favor, particularly if the underlying gets absolutely clubbed. After all, IEO can drop 60 percent, but DIG can't drop 120 percent.

Of course this is all little solace because it will always be outperformance of the "less bad" variety.

## How about Some Triples?

Needless to say, the math works even worse over time than the 2x shares. How about we throw some hypothetical energy 3x *to the extreme* shares into the above hypothetical nine-day move. There is actually a 3x energy ETF (symbol ERX) and a –3x (ERY), but we're just going to keep it hypothetical so we can still use DIG and DUG. (See Table 14.5.)

**Table 14.5**  Hypothetical Leveraged Energy ETF Trade

|  | IEO | DIG | IEO Bull 3x Shares | DUG | IEO Bear 3x Shares |
|---|---|---|---|---|---|
| Day 1, up 2% | 102 | 104 | 106 | 96 | 94 |
| Day 2, up 2% | 104.04 | 108.16 | 112.36 | 92.16 | 88.36 |
| Day 3, up 2% | 106.1208 | 112.4864 | 119.1016 | 88.4736 | 83.0584 |
| Day 4, up 2% | 108.243216 | 116.985856 | 126.247696 | 84.934656 | 78.074896 |
| Day 5, up 2% | 110.40808 | 121.66529 | 133.822558 | 81.5372698 | 73.3904022 |
| Day 6, down 2.45% | 107.70404 | 115.705802 | 123.990083 | 85.5311811 | 78.7826864 |
| Day 7, down 2.51% | 105 | 109.89534 | 114.651321 | 89.8259083 | 84.7164899 |
| Day 8, down 2.38% | 102.50 | 104.662229 | 106.461941 | 94.1033325 | 90.7676678 |
| Day 9, down 2.44% | 100 | 99.5567544 | 98.6720429 | 98.693739 | 97.4092045 |

You clearly see some extra gain if you own a triple and it trends a bit. But the retracements get significantly uglier, and the takeaway should be that those retracements compound upon themselves. So be forewarned.

## So What Should You Do with These Animals?

What do you, the trader or investor, do with these? There's almost two different, diametrically opposite answers here.

Let's start with what you, the investor, should not do—own them. Don't—for any considerable length of time. You can get a relative "win" only by correctly anticipating a multiday trend move. I'm not saying that this is impossible, just that it's very tough to do it with any consistency. And that's trading, not investing.

But by the same token, simply shorting both has risks too. Namely the allocation of capital changes as the underlying prices change.

Consider again the earlier DIG/DUG/IEO example. Suppose we short 100 shares of both DIG and DUG at $100, or a total of $10,000 allocated to each. At the time of entry, exposure to the energy stock space is zero, as the two exactly offset each other.

And then we have the initial five-day move wherein DIG has moved up to $121.66 and DUG has drifted to $81.54. Without doing a thing, the DIG position gets us short the equivalent of $24,332 of IEO (100 shares × the price of DIG × 2), while the DUG position gets us effectively long $16,308 IEO. Net them out, and a position that started out flat now has us short $8,024 worth of IYE.

Note something interesting about this behavior, a position that gets you shorter as the underlying (IEO) goes higher? Anyone? Anyone? Buehler?

Okay, I'll give the answer. It is tantamount to an options position in which you sell gamma. Yes positional gamma. Remember that all the way back in Chapter 2?

Like an options-generated short gamma position, you theoretically need to trade with the trend in order to stay flat. In other words, as IEO rallies, your position mandates that you do something bullish, perhaps buying IEO itself. This has the downside of course that if IEO reverses course and turns lower, you'll need to sell it back out at a loss to stay flat. So that dual drift in the ultras and inverses we noted above? The one that theoretically generated a profit via shorting both? The loss in IEO you realize may potentially eat that up, pending the specifics of timing.

But it's not exactly like an options position. Options have a fixed expiration date; you can pretty much plot on a graph how fast they will decay in value. In fact we did just that in Chapter 5. There's no such thing in the ultras and inverses, however. We know both sides will underperform at some juncture. We just don't know until after the fact how and why it gets there. This is an issue of path dependency. We can't necessarily plot it, so while we can call the behavior similar to options, we can't quite refer to it as identical.

## Size Matters

First things first. Let's get our sizing correct. The levered monsters remain very clear about your exposure, but investors get somewhat confused anyway. Let's look at these Russells for a second. As of early November 2008, we have the "regular" Russell ETF (IWM), a double long (UWM), and double short (TWM), a triple long (TNA), and a triple short.

Suppose you want the exposure of 1,000 shares long of IWM, but want to use one of the levered instruments. On November 12, 2008, IWM trades at about $45.80, so if we use UWM, we can buy 1,250 UWM at 18.30, short 178 TWM at 129, buy 443 shares of TNA at

34.50, or short 156 shares of TZA at 97.70 and accomplish the same thing.

How important is it to get the sizing right? Well consider the chart of TZA shown in Figure 14.9.

It sure looks like a one-year chart at first glance. I mean the stock lifted from 94 to 104, went back to 94, popped all the way to 114, and then went almost straight down to 72.50.

But believe it or not, that all happened in one day—November 13, 2008. That is the lightning in a bottle contained in leveraged ETFs. Handle with extreme care, if at all. This is Rule Numbers 1–10.

So let's tackle these in a disciplined manner. As a start, let's go back to our initial posture that we will not hold a long position for any important length of time in any of these mathematically challenged

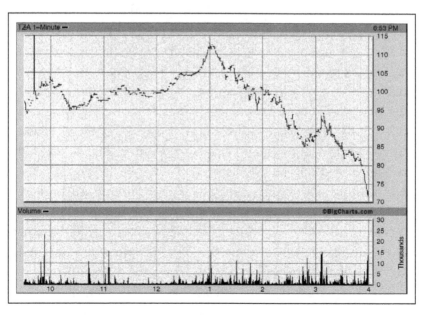

**Figure 14-9**   TZA, November 13, 2008 via BigCharts.com

derivative ETFs. However you slice it, you have the wind in your face owning them on a buy and hold sort of basis. It can work in short bursts, the same way you can kick a relatively short field goal into a breeze. But go longer in time (or move the ball back, if you like the analogy) and the decision tree must change.

So as an investor in the longer term, we'll do whatever we need to do to accomplish our goal. We're going to use the short delta. But then what's the best option? Shorting stock? Shorting calls? Or buying puts?

Much depends on your personal preferences. Are you comfortable with short gamma, a position that pays you money in the form of decay each day in return for getting you longer into dips and shorter into rallies (in the underlying)? Or do you like the reverse, long gamma, where you have the ammo to fade into moves but are under the pressure of doing it correctly?

Before you answer, keep something in mind—something we just went over. *Any* short delta position in an inverse or ultra has a modest short gamma component, again, thanks to the methodology of the tracking. So if you short calls in UWM, the effective position has a larger gamma exposure than shorting an equivalent position of IWM. This may work in your favor, of course. Let's say we put on a 30-day play, and IWM flops and chops and ends a cycle right back where it started. UWM will now almost certainly be lower than it was at the start. If you sold calls on Day 1 that were modestly ITM in both IWM and UWM, the IWM calls will still have some intrinsic value, whereas the UWMs may now be worthless.

This can also work against you. If IWM makes a trend move over the month, it's entirely possible that UWM overperforms on the up side. A call sell there will possibly outpace the IWM calls, to your detriment. So in a way, a call sale adds to a bet you are already making; that is, by shorting an inverse or ultra, you are betting modestly against volatility already.

## So what about buying puts?

Puts are often my vehicle of choice. But a put is a second bet on top of the directional bet against the inverse itself. It's a bet on the volatility of that move. And since these products move double or triple, the volatility you pay is double, or triple, as well. The plus side is that you don't have to buy too many to get some ammunition to flip stock in the underlying. The minus side is that you're paying daily decay and risking a decline in overall volatility, Same as a normal option. Yes, you get some benefit of the overall drift that we note earlier, but the volatility move more than offsets that.

Furthermore, in most cases, liquidity in inverses and ultras does not hold a candle to liquidity in the underlying options.

These are all things to consider when you're looking to enter a position in these products.

## What Can Go Wrong Can Go Very Wrong

It's not all peaches and cream, though. However you go about it, shorting one or both sides of an inverse/ultra combo has extreme risks of the unknown.

Consider the events of mid-September 2008, when the Treasury hastily instituted a ban on all short selling in financial stocks. As the plan was presented, there was some question over what stocks were banned and whether any party would get an exemption to the ban.

One such party was ProShares, or rather the unidentified third parties that physically short the shares that track the inverses. Remember ProShares itself does not go short, it does swaps.

But what if the third party can't short? Here's how ProShares responded:

Due to the emergency action announced by the Securities and Exchange Commission on September 18, 2008, temporarily prohibiting short sales of shares of certain financial companies, Short Financials ProShares (SEF) and UltraShort Financials ProShares (SKF) are not expected to accept orders from Authorized Participants to create shares until further notice. Unless notified otherwise, shares will be available for redemption by Authorized Participants as normal. The shares of these ProShares are expected to trade in the financial markets today, but may trade at prices that are not in line with their intraday indicative values.

And here's how SKF responded: It kept trading, but at a huge premium to net asset value. SKF closed 15 percent above in fact.

Fortunately for SKF shorts, an exemption came down the next day, and business and prices returned to normal. I bring this up to highlight that these are trading vehicles at their core and that there's always a potential surprise lurking around the corner, even on what seems like a locked trade.

Just for kicks, what if we throw around the exactly opposite idea—owning inverses or ultras or 3× shares against one another (say TNA vs. TZA) or against a basic ETF or a basket of stocks. You have the compounding wind in your face as we noted above, but you have a modest long gamma component that could maybe work for an active trader.

I emphasize *active*.

Here's the thought: What if you buy both TNA and TZA dollar neutral and then flatten out the dollars at the end of each day, using IWM, the Russell ETF. Let's adapt the above table yet again, using the same daily moves, but changing it to IWM and the tree of offshoots. Can we flip IWM well enough to offset the compounding drift?

For ease of explanation, we'll assume that IWM, TNA, and TZA all trade at $100. We're going to start long 1,000 shares each of TNA and TZA for a net long of $100,000 in each. Now suppose that on Day l the Russell rallies 2 percent. TNA goes to 106 and TZA to 94. We're now net long $12,000 worth of triples (106-94 × 1,000 shares), or $36,000 worth of IWM—or 352 shares.

Now let's say that on Day 2 IWM goes back down to 100, a dip of 1.9608 percent. Triple that and move the TNA and TZA accordingly, and we find that TNA closes at 99.76, for a loss of $240 on that position and that TZA closes at 99.53, for a loss of $470 or a net loss of $710. We did however earn $704 on the 352 shares of IWM for a net loss of $6, which is essentially zero when you count for rounding here and there. Move IWM up on Day 2, and you get similar nothing results.

So it's safe to conclude there's no there there in this trade.

## Can Math Solve This Hedging Problem?

What we've been talking about are all hypotheticals. What about some actual formulas? I put one of my Web site's sharper readers, "James W." on the task, and he came back with this analysis:

> The formula is derived from what would happen if you had a theoretical continuously adjusted double leveraged instrument. If you work through the math with calculus, the logarithmic moves will be twice as large. For the double long etf (*sic*), the total move over a long period of time will be the a^2 term. For the double short etf, the total long term will be the 1/a^2 term.
>
> The etfs are rebalanced daily. If they actually had continuously adjusted leverage and the index return was x, then the etf returns would be
>
> $(1 + x)^2 = 1 + 2x + x^2$
>
> $(1 - x)^2 = 1 - 2x + x^2$

so you have to subtract $x^2$ from the return for each etf every day. Now that I'm thinking about it some more, the inverse theoretical daily return would actually have to be

$$(1+x)^{-2} = 1 - 2x + 3x^2 - 4x^3 + \ldots$$

We can mostly ignore the $x^3$ and beyond terms, since even at a 10% daily move, $x^3 = .001$, and at a 5% move $x^3 = 1.25$bp.

So I should have had the formula with $-4v$ instead of $-2v$.

Then you have to add in the compounding effect of rebalancing. When the daily price movements are small, you get a reasonable approximation by just subtracting the variance with the right multiplier. But over long periods of time, or when price movements are large, that approximation is no longer any good.

It's easier to work out long periods or large movements if you convert back to logarithms. Up to about .02, $\log(1 + x) = x$ is a good approximation, but you really need to use $x - x^2/2$ for this case (which is good enough up to about .1, or a 5% daily move). The logarithms are:

Theoretical: $2x - x^2$ and $-2x - x^2$

Real: $2x - 2x^2$ and $-2x - 2x^2$

So both of them are underperforming by $x^2$ in a logarithmic sense every day. These errors you can actually just add up over time. Writing it out as the product of the theoretical instrument and the underperformance, the long-term result is

$$(a^2 + 1/a^2)(1 - v + v^2)$$

The variance for SPX in a normal year is about 6%, so the $v^2$ term can be ignored unless you are doing really long-term calculations or the volatility is particularly high. Another interesting consequence of this is that the theoretical instruments have a constant product. If you actually plot the product of a pair of double long and double short etfs, you get a graph that is slowly declining. Until September 2008, when most of the products started dropping rapidly. Many of them have lost half their value from the extreme volatility. Unfortunately, there is no way to trade the product of the price of two etfs.

If I had to summarize it all, I would say that the best advice is not to marry any of these products. Own them for a trade, but don't own them for an investment or a general portfolio hedge for any length of time. But by the same token, shorting both is not free money, unless you have some special insight as to when and where a move will reverse. If I maintain a position, I prefer running a short because I know at some juncture that I will have the wind at my back.

## If You're a Day Trader, Forget You Read the Last Four Sections

The best way to handle leveraged products is to keep things as simple as possible. Just day-trade them. Maybe hold them overnight if you have a strong opinion or need to own them. But don't go much beyond that with anything important.

They are complex. Keep it simple, I can't emphasize that enough.

Do I think the SEC should have ever allowed them to come to market? No, I don't. And in fact in the summer of 2009, FINRA issued a warning against holding leveraged ETFs, and firms such as UBS banned them from customer accounts.

Am I glad they came to market? You bet.

Leveraged ETFs are the best thing known to short-term traders. When I day-trade or swing-trade, I prefer volatility. And I prefer higher prices and lower quantities. And I'd rather have an "up" move. I don't short well; I trade too tightly. Leveraged inverses let me ride a short play "up" if I so choose.

Should that matter? I mean you can simulate whatever with or without these ETFs. So no, it shouldn't matter. But it eases the trade and the bet and lets me enter it simply in a form I like. So long live leveraged ETFs.

What about leveraged ETFs as far as individual investors are concerned? It's a huge disservice to list them without providing proper education. Major services like Barron's and Morningstar, to name a couple, didn't come out with all the caveats to owning these until about the end of 2008. And those were the good ones. Most all the others never bothered. And that's just wrong given the soaring popularity and obvious flaws in the buy and hold strategy.

## The Net Effect of These Leveraged Bets on the Marketplace

The year 2008 was a time of the never-ending blame game. People were looking to pin the collapse on something, anything, other than the actual bad actors creating and trading all the bad paper that ultimately did in many a bank. Shorts in general got their share of the blame, most notably as a by-product of the elimination of the plus tick rule, a topic we delve into in Chapter 15.

But these inverse leveraged ETFs and their soaring popularity took much of the heat as well. Was there any basis for this?

Let's look at a snapshot of one ugly day in the financials—February 17, 2009. Financial stocks, as measured by the ETF that tracks the Dow Jones Financial Index (IYF) were off by 4.27 percent.

SKF traded 32,778,100 shares and closed at 169.10. Accounting for the fact that each share bets on –2x the move in IYF, that represents a whopping $11,085,553,420 in market value of the financials transacted. Theoretically each trade can be offset by a basket of the component stocks, so we can translate that number into component shares.

In other words, if Bank XYZ comprises 10 percent of the index, than SKF trading theoretically accounts for $1,108,555,302 worth of XYZ trading. If $22 billion of XYZ itself traded, we could say that SKF volume accounted for about 5 percent of the total volume and XYZ. This would lead me to conclude that the mere existence of SKF did not have all that much impact on XYZ trading, especially since much of the SKF volume represents quick trades up and back and is never hedged with actual stocks.

Let's use real components of IYF. Table 14.6 shows the 10 largest components of IYF as of the close of February 17, 2009—the dollar amount of volume accounted for by SKF trading, the total dollar amount actually transacted, and the percent of volume accounted for by SKF.

There are some pretty stunning numbers in the right-hand column of the table. And they don't even account for FAZ, which traded 17,958,900 shares on February 17 and closed at $61.38. When you

**Table 14-6**   Percent of Stock Volume Accounted for by SKF Volume, 2/17/09

|     | Percent of IYF | Dollar Volume of 2/17 SKF | Volume on 2/17 | Closing Price | Actual Dollar Volume 2/17 | Percent of Actual Volume via SKF |
| --- | --- | --- | --- | --- | --- | --- |
| JPM | 8.99% | $996,591,252.46 | 91,310,300 | $21.65 | $1,976.867,995 | 50.41% |
| WFC | 5.98% | $662,916,094.52 | 122,067,500 | $13.69 | $1,671,104,075 | 39.67% |
| GS | 3.82% | $423,468,140.64 | 31,078,100 | $85.71 | $2,663,703,951 | 15.90% |
| BAC | 3.40% | $376,908,816,28 | 277,049,300 | $4.90 | $1.357,541,570 | 27.76% |
| BK | 2.93% | $324,806,715.21 | 17,416,400 | $23.13 | $402,841,332 | 80.63% |
| V | 2.69% | $298,201,387.00 | 8,895,400 | $54.25 | $482,575,450 | 61.79% |
| TRV | 2.55% | $282,681,612.21 | 7,945,000 | $39.17 | $311,205,650 | 90.93% |
| MS | 2.13% | $232,122,287.85 | 45,924,800 | $19.76 | $907,474,048 | 25.58% |
| USB | 2.05% | $227,253,845.11 | 51,758,000 | $10.73 | $555.363,240 | 40.92% |
| C | 1.85% | $205,082,738.27 | 192,101,700 | $ 3.06 | $587,831,202 | 34.89% |

triple that, it accounts for an additional $3,306,951,846 of financial stocks trading.

In other words, SKF and FAZ trading had completely dominated equity trading in the financial sector.

Now here, of course, are the caveats. This is an incredibly isolated example. There are "regular" ETFs in the space too, as well as bullish ones. So trades in these could be merely offset with other ETFs. In addition, these are truly trading products. I have never once hedged with a basket of actual financial stocks, and I doubt I am alone in this.

But still. If you are a conspiracy theorist and want to blame the mere existence of these leveraged monsters for, if nothing else, the rapidity of some declines, you certainly have your fodder based on these numbers.

## And Options

Now let's hop back to a question that arose earlier in the chapter. Do the mere presence and popularity of these products alter common options metrics? I mean from the last section, we can pretty much infer that they have an impact on volatility. But we could argue it both ways.

Unfortunately, it's a bit early in the life of these inverses to say anything definitive. But subjective logic suggests a big fat yes, their mere presence has a great impact.

It's a bet that replicates a hybrid between a future and a put option. An inverse owner now has ammunition to short puts in the underlying instrument. An SKF owner can sell puts in XLF and IYF, and perhaps any and all SPX and SPY derivatives. A QID owner can sell QQQQ puts, or INTC puts, or some other tech. And so on.

So presumably, higher inverse volume will beget higher put volume on the margins, but not necessarily a higher volatility index, such as the VIX or VXN. So perhaps the biggest effect will be the relationship between put/call readings and volatility readings.

And as the products get more popular, the ISE and CBOE will have to adjust for the fact that inverse puts *are* actually de facto calls, and likewise inverse calls are actually de facto puts. But we're a bit away just yet from that coming into play.

As to actual studies of the effect of these products, there are not a lot out there, and there's the problem that their rise in popularity corresponded to the ugliest of markets. There is some evidence, however slight, that they have taken some steam from actual VIX trading products.

I'll let my friend Bill Luby explain in a piece he penned in August 2008.

One year ago this month, VIX options peaked in popularity. As the graphic below [Figure 14.10] from IVolatility.com shows,

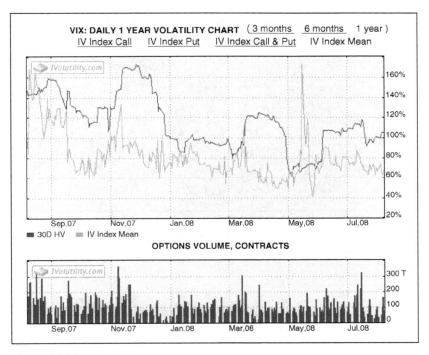

**Figure 14-10**

VIX options continue to trade at impressive volumes of about 100,000 contracts per day, but this number is about 30% below the levels from August–November of last year (2007).

Part of the reason for this change in trading patterns is that some of the portfolio hedging trades formerly conducted with VIX options are now being redirected to options on double inverse ETFs. Back in February, in Interest in VIX Waning? I spoke about how the new trend seemed to favor QID options over VIX options. Six months later, the popularity of QID and SDS options persists, with QID + SDS options now accounting for approximately one third of the volume in VIX options. [See Figures 14.11 and 14.12.]

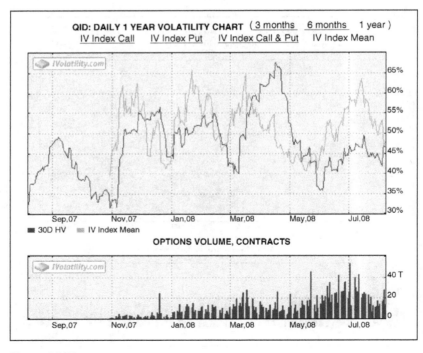

**Figure 14-11**

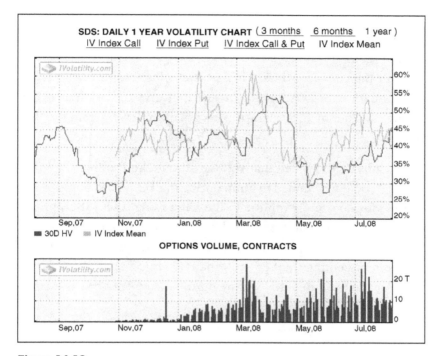

**Figure 14-12**

More recently, the rise of double inverse sector ETF options has translated into more choices for investors and lower market share for the VIX. While sector options are more likely than VIX options to be used for speculative purposes than as portfolio hedges, the surge in options volume for double inverse sector ETFs is worth highlighting here, with the SKF (double inverse sector ETF for financials) and DUG (double inverse sector ETF for oil and gas) receiving the most interest.

Unfortunately, we don't have a "control" market to compare everything to. These products came down the pike at a unique moment in market history, on the front end of a historic financial meltdown. And they got incredibly popular in a year where the VIX ranged from the mid-teens to near 100.

And again, it's still early.

Over the course of time, I believe we will get some good metrics from the inverses themselves—excessive inverse and/or ultra volume relative to other metrics, along the lines of the following from Dr. Brett Steenbarger.

> A while back, I noted that volume among the ProShares Ultra S&P 500 ETFs tended to jump during market selloffs. I updated this view to express volume in the Ultra Long ETF (SSO) plus volume in the Ultra Short ETF (SDS) as a function of total NYSE volume (light line above). As we can see from the dark line representing the S&P 500 Index itself (SPY), we've seen a steady increase in Ultra volume during the recent decline, with

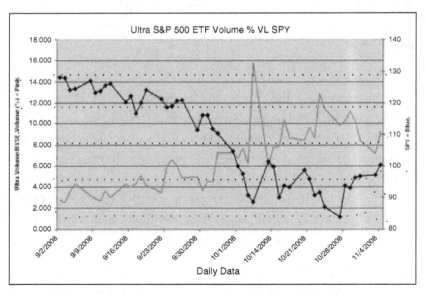

**Figure 14-13**

a particularly notable spike in mid-October, when we hit a peak in the number of stocks making new 52-week lows.

Interestingly, the volume in SDS and SSO as a proportion of SPY volume rose from about 13% in early September to over 30% during the last two weeks. Moreover, if we look at yesterday's volume among all North American ETFs, Ultra funds occupied three of the top eight positions.

Because the Ultra funds are double-size relative to other index ETFs, they are excellent tools for assessing speculative activity in the stock market. What we've tended to see, when we correct for an ongoing rise in the popularity of the Ultra shares, is enhanced speculative activity when markets correct and a relative drying up of such activity as markets top out. From the perspective of sentiment, this may be a nice measure of market emotionality: fear/greed versus complacency.

## What Have We Learned

Inverses are here, they're real, and they're going to stay. There's strong evidence that they have taken steam, not to mention volume, from a host of other derivative products.

Tread very carefully when using them. It's like getting on a scary roller coaster. You know going in the double and triple volatility will turn you inside out and upside down as you get on the ride, but you don't really know how it feels until you try it.

And whatever you do, don't get tempted to hold these for the long haul either as an investment or a general hedge. They *will* disappoint.

But by all means trade them, use them. Swing trading/day trading, anything short term in nature works fine. But again, discipline is more key here than in a normal product because the compounding will destroy the trade if you let it fester.

# Chapter 15

# CHARTIN' THEM
# DERIVATIVES

A ll things leverage have indeed become all the rage. At least that was the case in 2008 as discussed in the last chapter.

But this doesn't mean that you can or should chart them—or other derivatives for that matter.

In December 2008, Eric Oberg, a former managing director at Goldman Sachs with experience in fixed income, currencies, and commodities, penned a series of articles for *RealMoney Silver* on the subject of leveraged ETFs. In response to a reader question regarding traditional technical analysis on leveraged ETFs, he offered this opinion on technical analysis of these products:

> OK—this will be a little roundabout, but I think I'll get there, so please bear with me. First off, I believe technical analysis is important because others think it is important (kind of like how Paris Hilton is famous . . . for being famous!). But I do not believe it is the be-all and end-all—particularly when it comes to derivatives. And indices are derivatives. One of the very first things I learned at Goldman as a trainee was: "Securities are linear, but options are curvy." What that means is that stock prices

will follow a linear path, but derivatives follow an exponential path, given the math of the price function.

So if key technical levels are based on a linear path, but all of the sudden you introduce something turbo-charged, you can blow right through a support/resistance level without even knowing it or contemplating the level. Thus, these levels can be manipulated. If I bought up the short index, knowing that the swap counterparty was going to have to hedge, and at the same time started shorting the underlying stocks, I can create two, three, four times the selling pressure. (The same thing goes the other way with the long funds.)

Again, because these ETFs segregate bears and bulls, we never realize true price discovery—this is compounded, because the volume in these sector ETFs can swamp the volume in the underliers. All this adds up to potential for market manipulation—manipulation of levels once deemed sacrosanct.

As a second part to this answer, I mentioned that indices are themselves derivatives. The composition of an index, particularly market-cap-weighted indices, varies over time. The composition of the S&P 500 in 2000 is very different from the composition today. So why is a level we hit in 2000 relevant to me now? Or even closer to home, in the financials index, Lehman and Bear, I am sure, were components at the beginning of the year but are nowhere to be found now. So looking at the index level in January vs. the index level in December is not really an apples-to-apples comparison.

So it is downright laughable to me when I see people talking about technical levels on these levered ETFs—we are talking about a derivative on a derivative (and think about options on these things—we are talking about derivatives cubed). How on earth could one think that a technical level has any validity whatsoever when we look at prices of the levered ETFs themselves

when so much is going on with the underliers, the index composition, the NAV distortions, the short volatility play, etc.?
Unless the person telling you about these technical levels on
levered ETFs holds a Ph.D. in nuclear physics, don't listen.
And as a hint, Ph.D.s in nuclear physics generally don't believe
in voodoo.

Oberg makes an interesting point regarding the charting of derivatives.
And one I agree with. You simply can't apply the same rules you do
to a normal stock or index or ETF if you go beyond one day. These
are derivatives that reset every day. There's no such thing as low or
high in absolute price. They begin every day with a clean slate.

Take the chart of IYF with a 20-day and 50-day MA in the final
quarter of 2008 shown in Figure 15.1.

And now compare it to its wildly popular -2x evil tracking friend,
SKF. (See Figure 15.2.)

**Figure 15-1**  IYF: October–December 2008, via StockCharts.com

**Figure 15-2** SKF, October–December 2008, via StockCharts.com

Even if you flip the SKF chart upside down, many odd disparities become apparent as you relate the two. SKF hits "support" a little under 120 on October 13 and then again on November 3. IYF, however, hit 60 the first time, and 55 the second time. By the time SKF gets back to "support" again on December 5, IYF is below 50.

The price of 120 in SKF means three very different things in a time span of less than two months.

Enjoy simple technicals? IYF spends the whole time under its 50-day MA, while SKF flits around it several times, and basically spends half the quarter above and half below.

You can make the case that SKF has become the "dog" and IYF (and XLF for that matter) the "tail." And thus SKF has become the right chart, whatever that means. But I'd note that this makes almost no sense. It tracks an ETF that tracks an index that tracks a basket of financial stocks. But it's like a game of telephone at this point because

SKF has become just an animal on it's own with no real relationship to the underlying stocks over any significant time frame.

But that's not the issue. Rather, it's whether taking something that's already a derivative (IYF) and using standard charting techniques and then applying those same techniques to a derivative of that derivative will yield anything resembling an apples-to-apples comparison. And the evidence suggests that it doesn't. You have two different animals; you need two different sets of rules.

And I remain unconvinced that you can apply any rule to a leveraged ETF. A one-directional short-term move in the underlying results in a compounded directional move in the leveraged derivative. Volatility ultimately produces longer-term underperformance as we note in Chapter 13. And so on. It's vaguely similar to trying to chart a call option. Each successive time a stock revisits a price, the call will almost certainly trade lower thanks to time decay. If it doesn't, it's because of some presumably large uptick in volatility. What would a chart on this option tell you? Something disparate and misleading no doubt.

## So How About the Ultimate Derivative of a Derivative?

The ultimate derivative of a derivative? Of course, I refer to the VIX.

Does the same way that SKF of 120 means different things at different times apply to the VIX? Can we apply standard charting techniques and get meaningful results? Can you relate a VIX at one time to a VIX at the same level but at a different time?

I'd suggest the answers to the above are yes and no and yes and no.

A basic chart can indeed give an excellent picture of what's going on with volatility. For instance, let's highlight the regimelike longer-term nature of volatility. Figure 15.3 shows the VXO from mid 1993 to the end of 1996.

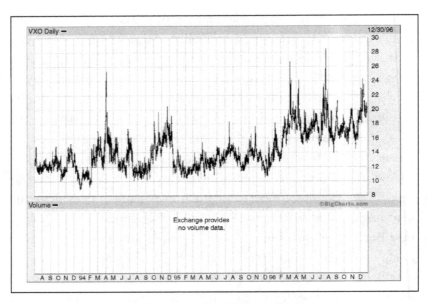

**Figure 15-3** VXO July 1993–December 1996, via BigCharts.com

The illustration shows that pretty much nothing is happening, certainly into the end of 1995. Aside from one very brief blip all the way to the mid 20s, the VXO hovered between 10 and the high teens forever. In fact it spent almost the entirety of 1995 between 12 and 15. Then 1996 came, and the VXO lifted a bit, into the high teens for the most part. This seemed like just a high end of the general range.

How about we change regimes to the late 1990s. Irrational exuberance. Asian and Russian debacles in 1998. The Internet. The tech bubble. The tech bubble implosion. It's a regular Billy Joel song breaking out, minus the rhymes.

Figure 15.4 shows the VXO from 1997 through mid 2003.

In hindsight, 1996 turned into a transition year to the thrombolic moves of the late 1990s. New "normal" VXO had become mid 20s versus mid teens in the earlier 1990s. The blowoffs were now in the 40s and 50s.

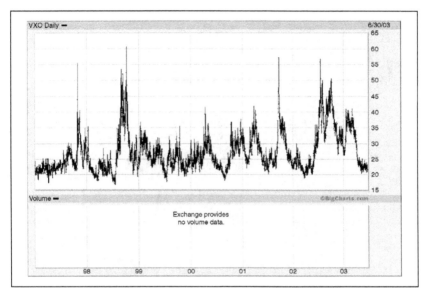

**Figure 15-4**   VXO January 1997–June 2003, via BigCharts.com

But alas all good things (or bad things) must come to an end. Money everywhere. The Fed flooded the system with liquidity. Refi mania. And volatility partying like it was 1993 again. (See Figure 15.5.)

Yes, by mid 2005, volatility had effectively gone back to a large shoe size.

So let's get back to the original questions.

You can see that a basic chart has some value; it certainly provides a bigger-picture look. And a sense of that mean we always hear the VIX is reverting to.

But by the same token, the VXO does not behave at all like a stock. It's a statistic. It has a floor, probably something around 9 or 10. It doesn't have a ceiling per se, but it does have levels where it trades only in very unusual market action.

And most importantly, it does not have supply/demand characteristics like a stock. Let's say conceptually that someone "got long volatil-

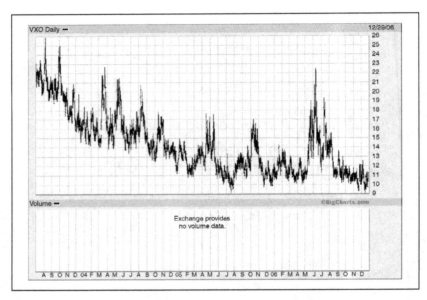

**Figure 15-5** VXO July 2003–December 2006, via BigCharts.com

ity" at a 30 VIX. He does that by purchasing actual options on SPX futures. And those options work in the general sense if realized SPX volatility from the time of purchase to the time of sale (or expiration) is higher than what he paid. In other words, he can top out implied volatility with his purchase, sell it back out 10 points lower, and make money *if* the index itself is sufficiently volatile.

In an extreme case, there may barely even be a trade at a given VIX. Take January 22, 2008. The market gapped down huge after a long holiday weekend. The VIX "opened" at 37, thanks to some very wide and very high quotes in OTM puts on the SPX (we describe the VIX calculation procedure in Chapter 3). But within a couple of minutes, the market stabilized, offers got realistic, and volatility caved. And of course, the pundits declared that 37 was some sort of key VIX level, which of course, made no sense. It was a number on a screen that coincided with what turned into a market bottom for a few months.

In a sense, there's no particular significance if the VIX revisits an old price, makes a new high or low, and so on. In another sense, there's great significance psychologically if you believe in a self-fulfilling prophecy. It's logical to assume that there is some support or resistance in the actual market when a subset of players sees a VIX chart point approaching. So while I do find it a bit nonsensical, I can't completely discount the notion of VIX charting.

## So How Would I Chart the VIX?

How to chart the VIX? I would stick to near-term and moving average analysis. As I note above, absolute numbers can have some importance, despite all logic, but I would not rely on them if there's much time lapse. The bottom line is that while 30 VIX may mean something to somebody if it happened a month ago, it bears little resemblance to whatever a 30 VIX might have meant a year or three years or a decade ago.

Consider the following changes in the marketplace during the 13.5 year timeframe covered in Figures 15.3, 15.4 and 15.5.

In 1993, we had volume a fraction of what we see in 2008. Listed stocks effectively traded in one spot, the NYSE. Nasdaq automation consisted of (as we know in hindsight) market makers keeping their quotes artificially wide. Stocks traded in eighths. And the first ETFs— the SPY and the DIA—just started trading and had little impact. Most options were singly listed on one exchange. There was relatively little in the way of automation.

By the late 1990s and the early "aught's," you could execute an options trade from the comfort of your house. The first all-automated options exchange, the ISE had opened up shop. Pretty much any option with any measurable volume traded on multiple exchanges. Stocks now changed hands in pennies.

By 2008, many options also traded in pennies. We have ETFs for everything. And leveraged inverse ETFs. And no plus tick rule for short sells.

I mention all this because each and every one of these developments has had some meaningful, but not perfectly quantifiable, effect on volatility. I would suggest that decimalization decreased volatility on the margins. We now had more price points. If nothing else, this narrowed down the range of block trades. Likewise, I believe automation reduces volatility, as it's much simpler to hold tight, knowing you can bounce out of a position with a mouse click, than it is wondering if it might take you an hour to trade something, assuming that someone even answers the phone.

Conversely, ETFs have probably increased volatility as the baskets used to offset them lead to greater correlation between stocks and sectors.

The point is that market developments over the course of time change the nature and dynamics of trading. And this must necessarily pull and tug at volatility, altering what is fair and normal for the VIX at any given time. Thus an absolute number in the VIX, any number, today means something completely different from what it did 5, 10, or 15 years ago.

Long story short, I would certainly stick with shorter-term analysis.

## Study Time

TradingMarkets.com has a pretty simple VIX guideline—The TradingMarkets 5% Rule.

The 5% rule states—Do not buy stocks (or the market) anytime the VIX is 5% below its moving average. Why? Because since 1989, the S&P 500 cash market has "lost" money on a net basis

5 days following the times the VIX has been 5% below its 10 day ma. That's right, in spite of the S&P 500 rising over 300% since 1989, it's lost money 5 days following the VIX closing 5% or more below its 10 day ma.

The TradingMarkets 5% Rule is also extremely powerful on the buy side. Since 1989, whenever the VIX has been 5% or more above its 10 day ma, the S&P 500 has achieved returns which are better than 2 1/2 to 1 compared to the average weekly returns of all weeks.

What does this mean for you? It means the potential edge lies in buying the market and stocks when the VIX is at least 5% above its 10 day ma, and to lock in gains (and also not buy) when the VIX is 5% or more below its 10 day ma.

Sounds great, but is it actually as good as meets the eye? CXO Advisory studies the problem, and says no.

The following chart (Figure 15.6) reproduces the TradingMarkets analysis. The average return for the S&P 500 index for all five trading-day intervals in the sample is 0.19%, with standard deviation 2.14%. The average return for the five trading-day holding intervals after 5% relative high (low) VIX rule signals is 0.49% (−0.02%), with standard deviation 2.45% (1.96%). Taken at face value, these results confirm the TradingMarkets conclusions. Note that actual volatility is higher (lower) than normal after high (low) VIX signals.

Is there any economic value in these results? In other words, are there any trading strategies here?

There are two issues with constructing trading strategies from these results:

1. Standard deviations are large compared to the differences in mean returns. A trader must therefore systematically trade the

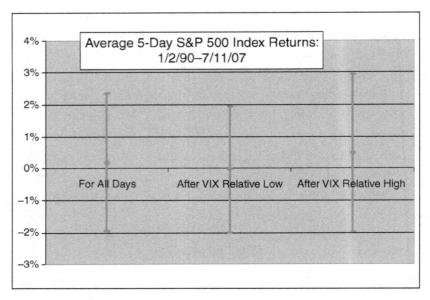

**Figure 15-6**

signals many, many times (say >100) to cancel out the variability and achieve the indicated mean returns reliably. Short-term technical signals typically have this drawback.

2. More critically, because the signals frequently come in bunches or streaks, there is a problem with the calculation of mean returns. In fact, there are more trading signals than there are five trading-day intervals in the sample. From a statistical perspective, there is serial correlation bias because returns for some days are included in more than one signaled holding interval. From a practical perspective, a trader cannot systematically act on all the signals because many signals occur while funds are still committed based on a prior signal.

To resolve the second problem, we eliminate streaks by thinning the signals such that no two signals fall within five trading days of each other. Specifically, we default to the first signal after any five trading-day gap and ignore any signals in the subsequent five trading days. This thinning reduces the number of high-VIX signals from 1,246 to 492, and the number of low-VIX signals from 1,080 to 364. The next chart (Figure 15.7) shows the results. The mean return for the five trading days after high VIX signals falls from 0.49% to 0.25%, while the return after low VIX signals rises from –0.02% to 0.11%. Imposing an executable trading strategy therefore eliminates most of the anomaly identified by TradingMarkets.

How would trading on the thinned subsample of high-VIX signals compare to buy-and-hold?

Who's right? Both, really.

TradingMarkets has a valid rule there. But as CXO shows, it's not necessarily possible to trade off it. To me, it would be best to use all of

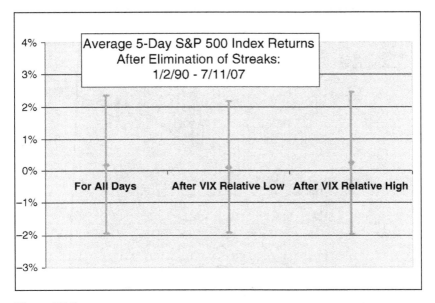

**Figure 15-7**

it as more a guideline and less an actionable indicator. In fact, I prefer looking at it backwards. Instead of actually trading when the VIX breaks one barrier or another, I observe how the market behaves at such junctures. I find that this gives decent clues to the intermediate trend.

In other words, let's say the VIX lifts 10 percent or more above the 10-day SMA. And the market turns up pretty quickly. That's telling me we're in a solid intermediate trend, and I want to look to fade any general market weakness. Conversely, what if you have a stretch like this—September and October 2008? (See Figure 15.8.)

Depending on what threshold you use, you get pretty long pretty often into an SPY stock chart that ended up looking like the chart shown in Figure 15.9.

Basically, a disaster. However, just simply looking backwards, you would have noticed pretty early on that the extended VIX just begat more selling in the market. And caution was the best action.

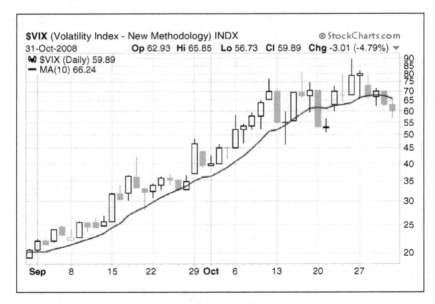

**Figure 15-8** VIX, September–October 2008, via StockCharts.com

**Figure 15-9** SPY, September–October 2008, via StockCharts.com

But of course, fall of 2008 was an outlier. And hindsight is 20/20. I just use these graphs as an example of the danger of reading too much into all this.

Here's something to watch for though—a countertrend move in volatility within a trend. As in the perpetually lifting volatility graph above, check out that blip way below the SMA on October 20 and 21. In hindsight, it gave a good market sell signal in a countertrend rally.

Let's now look at the ensuing two months. The VIX is shown in Figure 15.10. And the SPY is shown in Figure 15.11.

You've got another good countertrend sell signal on the volatility chart in early November. But then in late November quite the opposite as the dip in volatility portended *not* a time to sell, but rather a change in overall market character.

**Figure 15-10**    VIX, November–December 2008, via StockCharts.com

**Figure 15.11**    SPY, November–December 2008, via StockCharts.com

So my point would be, as experience and statistical evidence from CXO show, this indicator is pretty much hit or miss insofar as tradable signals go. But it does yield some interesting info in regard to sentiment and intermediate market trends.

## Summary

Many great minds have tackled technical analysis and provided us with boundless insight.

But we have to be careful to not lazily apply what we learn there into asset classes that do not actually behave as stocks do, like derivatives such as the inverses and of course volatility indices.

While we can debate the significance of a given absolute price in a stock or an index as it gets revisited, we really can't debate it in a derivative. It has little significance beyond it being a small psychological component.

If anyone ever says something like, "The market always rallies when the VIX hits 'X'," run, don't walk, away. This person has a very misinformed opinion.

Moving average analysis can yield some better results, but even there exercise extreme caution. Use it more as a thermometer of the market's overall temperature than as a trading indicator.

# Chapter 16

# PLUS TICKS AND OTHER RULES

As we note in Chapter 14, we rarely go long without some sort of new market rule or technological advance that changes the nature of trading and makes market comparisons across eras a somewhat dubious task. This is especially true when it comes to something like volatility.

The year 2007 proved no different. And options and volatility principles played a central role in the whole saga.

In July 2007, the SEC eliminated the plus tick rule. Within 18 months, such stalwart financial firms as Countrywide, Bear Stearns, AIG, Lehman Brothers, and Washington Mutual, not to mention Fannie Mae and Freddie Mac, ceased to exist. Actually they existed but as a shell absorbed into a better-heeled former rival—or as a ward of the government.

And the world rushed to assign cause and effect. According to the critics, elimination of the plus-tide rule caused spiraling Bear raids, which essentially caused a self-fulfilling prophecy cycle. Not that Jim Cramer was the most vocal critic of the rule change, but he does express a widely held belief as well documented in this recap of a Mad Money episode on March 20, 2008.

The damage the market's suffered since the U.S. Securities and Exchange Commission repealed the uptick rule last summer is undeniable, Cramer said during Thursday's Mad Money, and regulators need to admit their mistake.

Cramer's not blaming the Dow's decline to 12,361 from 13,577 solely on the SEC's decision, but the size, severity and even savageness of the declines we've seen since July are without question the product of this new open season for short-selling, he said.

So what is this uptick rule? After the short-selling bear raids that caused the crash of 1929 and the endless knockdown of stocks that followed, regulators required that there be a buyer willing to pay more for a stock than the last sale, known as an uptick, before that stock could be sold short. Basically, a stock had to go up a bit before it could be brought down.

That rule stayed in effect for almost 80 years until July, 6, 2007, when the SEC got rid of it. Hedge funds lobbied for a repeal, and the feds conceded after a test proved life without the uptick would be just fine. Of course, that test took place during a bull market, where a bear raid would never happen, and not an environment like the one we have now where raids are rampant.

No wonder the SEC didn't think the sharp declines caused by bear raids could happen in today's market. They claimed smaller spreads, higher liquidity and greater transparency would prevent such drastic downturns. But spreads don't matter, Cramer said, and that liquidity, courtesy of a brokerage credit crisis, has disappeared.

The SEC also said that "regulatory surveillance" will "reduce the risk of undetected manipulation." But, as Cramer pointed out, it's too late by the time regulators get involved. Bear raids destroy confidence, taking the stock even lower, then the self-fulfilling nature of the declines gets reinforced when investors assume the company's going out of business, causing a run, much like what happened to Bear Stearns.

So the SEC's "recreated exactly what happened in the 1930s in this country," Cramer said. "The cause and effect is real."

So he called for a return to the uptick rule, for the sake of individual investors everywhere. After all, when a multibillion-dollar hedge fund is selling short 500,000 shares of a stock, shareholders are helpless.

"We will not have peace in the markets until [the uptick rule] is restored," Cramer said.

This all begs the question, does any of this reflect the reality of short selling in 2007 when the rule was repealed? There's little dispute about the twin facts that the plus tick rule went away in mid 2007 and that the market had a historically rough go of it in 2008. But that does not necessarily mean a causality there. We had other things going on, such as a real estate collapse and an implosion in the value of mortgage paper on the books of virtually every financial institution. And so on.

Michael Steinhart of Hedge Fund and Hedgefolios fame takes the opposite viewpoint.

Here's my Uptick Uptake, I don't care which argument is right or wrong. I deal with the rules that are in place right now.

There are many market forces and identifying one or the other as a primary cause of total market movement is very simplistic and dangerously ignorant. The idea that the uptick rule would have prevented us from declining a whopping 15% off the record high is absurd. I tend to place more emphasis for the selloff on the credit crisis, declining corporate profitability and the general contraction in the economy. Those seem to be pretty fair reasons for a market decline if you ask me.

But rather than just messing around debating specific reasons why bulls are having the wealth they feel entitled to "stolen" from them, why don't we just skip past all that and prevent anyone from selling a stock for any reason? Of course I am kidding, but that would certainly accomplish the record highs the bulls want back. Why stop at reinstating the uptick rule to supposedly end the market's problems? Why not just ban short selling altogether? That's been debated before and has actually happened in some places. How did that work out?

And later of course we did briefly try the whole short-banning idea with predictably nothing positive to show for it.

Personally, I lean more toward the Steinhart viewpoint if for no other reason than the rule had become outdated, and of all the other constraints on shorting, having to find a plus tick morphed into about the easiest rule to work around.

In order to short a stock in the United States, we first must arrange to borrow shares to short. In theory, we must satisfy this step before it even gets to the whole plus tick issue. And in theory, this should act as a circuit breaker in and of itself.

But moving from theory to fact, alas it didn't. For as the light of day shined on the whole stock-shorting world, we learned that arranging a borrow, or that you might get a borrow, or that you have a hunch you might get a borrow someday, was sufficient to actually sell shares short. Stock loans provided a cash cow for both sell-side Wall Street that collected spreads on it and buy-side Wall Street that actually owned the shares and earned de facto dividends on them via lending them out.

Remember Bialystock and Bloom selling countless 10 percent shares of their play in the movie *The Producers*? That's what we had with stock loans as many of the same Wall Street firms that would later cry foul at all the shorting would abet the alleged "enemy" by lending out the same shares several times over.

So with rampant lack of observance of this rule, it escapes me why someone expected that the "protection" of the plus tick rule would save the day. I mean, quite simply, if shorting never-borrowed stock was so commonplace, why would that short then say, "Wait, I would never stoop so low as to not wait for a plus tick, which, with multiple markets and penny trading, is almost impossible to define in 2007."

But look, I am not here to defend shorts or ascribe blame for the 2008 collapse of the financials. What I am here to do though is demonstrate how market developments over the years turned a 70-year-old rule into essentially the Edsel of regulations.

## So I Want to Make a Bearish Bet on a Stock. Do I Need to Physically Short It?

The short answer (no pun intended) is a big, resounding no.

How else could a large and sophisticated player make a bearish bet on a stock? Well she could probably just call her covering (clearing) firm and tell the firm that she wants to go short X amount of stock XYZ. Then the firm will tell the player, "Done." Then someone at the firm will worry about actually executing the transaction in house. A decade or so ago this person could just trade a "bullet" wherein the firm let him go long stock and long deep puts for parity as part of a one-shot execution.

But since I don't know for a fact that this happened, how about looking at some other ways she can make an identical bearish bet to actually shorting XYZ, using only listed products.

She can buy XYZ puts.

She can buy XYZ puts and short XYZ calls.

She can buy XYZ puts and short calls on the exact same strike and expiration (a synthetic, please see Chapter 12) and have virtually exactly the same position she would have if she shorted stock.

She can buy deep puts and stock (generally known as married puts), and then bang out her long stock.

Let's say XYZ is a financial stock, since that's where all the shorting rancor took place. The player can short an ETF like the XLF or IYF and then buy the component stocks in the ETF that she does not want to short.

Want to ban shorting ETFs too (that happened briefly in October 2008)? She can buy an inverse leveraged ETF like SKF or FAZ and to get double or triple the fun and again, buy the component stocks she doesn't want to be short. I would note though that banning shorts on an ETF but allowing an inverse ETF to exist makes less than no sense.

She can sell broader index futures or index ETFs and buy back the stocks she does not want to short.

She can short single stock futures.

The point here is not to recommend any or all of these plays. Many (probably most) are practical only for a certain sized operation. The point here is to demonstrate that in a world of options and ETFs and inverse ETFs, actual physical shorting of stock means little. You want to bet bearishly on a name? You will never need to find out the phone number for a stock loan.

## How Does This Affect You, the Smallish Investor or Trader?

So what impact does this have on you? Let's go back to the first paragraph of Mr. Steinhart's passage: "Here's my Uptick Uptake, I don't care which argument is right or wrong. I deal with the rules that are in place right now."

Whether you think the whole debate around the plus tick rule is a convenient red herring to distract from bigger issues (my personal take) or not, we should agree on one thing. We can't ever make the rules of the game exactly as we would like them. I wish that we never dually listed options, and I wish that we still traded them in eighths. I liked my niche as an AMEX market maker under those conditions. Unfortunately, no one consulted with me before changing the rules of the game.

You may find abolition of the plus tick rule the worst crime against humanity, and you may have done your part to make your feelings known. This is certainly admirable. As of this writing, it did look as though it was coming back someday in same revised form. But until it does, the only logical choice involves dealing with the rules that exist.

What would that entail with respect to the plus tick rule?

Well, you could probably make the case that it adds to volatility on the margins—on both "margins" I would note. It logically produces a bit more downside to a move already in progress if for no other reason than it does make it easier for shorts to pile on.

But by the same token, the easier the shorting and the greater the quantity of shorting, the more players get trapped when the worm turns and the stock everyone "knows" has a value of zero all of a sudden heads higher. All of which has the effect of providing more upside juice.

So my strong advice is to forget about fighting the battle over whether we should have this rule and concentrate on the battle of trading in a world where plus tick protection does not exist. Over the course of time, an average VIX reads in the 19 or 20 range. Perhaps with no plus tick rule, that range will tweak a bit higher. Instead of complaining, try adjusting. Widen stops a smidge so as not to get shaken out by noise. Widen price targets as well. Reduce position sizing.

# INDEX

CPSIA information can be obtained
at www.ICGtesting.com
Printed in the USA
LVHW011338060121
675608LV00004B/12